Study Guide for

SOCIOLOGY
THIRD EDITION

by Rodney Stark

Carol A. Mosher
Jefferson Community College

Wadsworth Publishing Company
Belmont, California
A Division of Wadsworth, Inc.

Printed in the United States of America   49

1   2   3   4   5   6   7   8   9   10—93   92   91   90   89

ISBN   0-534-09602-6

Contents

How to Use This Study Guide

This study guide is designed to aid your study of the third edition of Rodney Stark's SOCIOLOGY. It is meant to complement the text, not substitute for it. The text is well written and contains a common thread that ties the chapters together; you will find it informative and lively reading. But even with a well-written text, students sometimes find it difficult to focus their study effectively and ferret out the most important information. This study guide will assist you in this process.

There is no foolproof way to study and no one way to use this study guide. This guide might be used in any (or all) of the following ways:

1. Before you read each chapter, the study guide can alert you to the key concepts, theories, and research studies discussed in the chapter. This preview will enable you to focus your attention effectively.
2. Throughout your reading and study, it can reinforce your knowledge of important topics.
3. After you complete each chapter, it can serve as a review and self-test to ensure that you understand the most important material.
4. Prior to an exam, it can serve as a review and refresher, alerting you to areas that may need further study.

You will want to develop a system that works best for you. Your professor or other students may be able to offer additional suggestions for effective use.

Format of the Study Guide

The text is divided into five parts, each containing between two and five chapters. (Individual professors may deviate from this format when designing courses.) Chapters in the study guide are grouped together to follow a format similar to that in the text but allow flexibility in the event of any deviation.

The study guide's twenty-one chapters correspond directly to the chapters in the text. Each chapter contains the following:

1. An overview that briefly highlights the main topics contained in the chapter.
2. A capsule summary that condenses the chapter into a few paragraphs. Key topics and concepts are printed in bold type for easy reference.
3. A listing of key concepts. In addition, most chapters list key theories, research studies, and figures, with specific page references for key concepts and research studies. These form the basis of sociology and sociological inquiry, and a thorough knowledge of them is essential for mastery of the material.

4. Completion, or fill-in-the-blank, questions that are drawn from all aspects of the chapter. The answers appear at the end of the chapter.

5. Multiple-choice questions that cover the entire chapter. Again, the answers are provided at the end of the chapter.

6. Essay questions that require a synthesis and application of the important material. Many of these use the key words described in the section on how to study. The first two essays in each chapter reflect the cognitive levels described in the introductory section on essay questions.

Following each group of chapters is a brief review of the chapters plus a suggestion for a special project designed to offer some creative ways of actually putting sociology to use with the information gained in that section. The directions for these projects are open-ended to allow flexibility and creativity and are meant as suggestions rather than specific assignments. You should consult your instructor for advice and direction before undertaking these projects. In addition, this study guide contains a short section on study techniques, describing some strategies for effective study and test taking. It is designed to be useful not only in your sociology course but in other college courses as well. Many of the completion and essay questions contained in this guide apply some of these techniques.

Of course, study guides do have some limitations. No study guide can ever substitute for a thorough reading and comprehensive study of a text. That is not the purpose of a study guide, nor should it be. Many professors cover additional material in lectures, which obviously cannot be included in this guide; similarly, outside readings are often assigned, which must be studied separately. Occasionally, an individual professor may emphasize a specific area in the text in greater depth than it is treated here. This guide should be used as a resource and study aid, but it should not be relied on as the only tool for effective study. Nevertheless, this guide should assist you in your study and help you to appreciate the challenge and excitement of sociology.

Acknowledgments

I would like to thank Rodney Stark for asking me to write this study guide and Sheryl Fullerton, Sharon McNally, and Wadsworth Publishing Company for their assistance with this project. In addition I thank Christi Rowan for her editorial assistance and support.

The section on using the SQ4R method was written by Nancy Hoover, academic dean at Jefferson Community College. She willingly let me include it here. Sarah Dye, of Elgin Community College, provided me with extensive material on test-taking techniques. The section on effective test taking is drawn from her material. In addition Margo Elliott, associate professor of psychology, wrote the section entitled "Essay Questions: Understanding Format" and helped write the essay questions. I am indebted to these colleagues for their information and assistance.

Carol Mosher

Studying a Text: The SQ4R Method

Nancy Hoover
Academic Dean
Jefferson Community College

Author's Note

Success in sociology or any other college course depends, in part, on your ability to study effectively. Good study techniques allow you to make the most of your study time and can ultimately lead to a better understanding of course material and better grades. Although no method of study works for all students in all courses, experts on study skills have devised several techniques that have proved successful. Of course, no study technique can compensate for failure to attend classes or failure to complete assigned work. These techniques can, however, allow you to retain more information and use your study time more effectively.

Many students, particularly freshmen, simply do not know how to study. They complain that they spend many hours studying, yet they perform poorly on exams and other assignments. I can appreciate their position since, as a freshman, I spent many hours trying to memorize whole passages from texts the night before an exam only to find that I had missed much of the important information and had forgotten most of what I had memorized. True, I had spent many hours studying, but they were, for the most part, wasted. I simply did not know how to study effectively. Once I learned basic study techniques, I actually spent fewer hours studying, yet I learned more and received better grades.

This section offers some strategies for effective study by describing the SQ4R method for studying texts and providing suggestions for taking objective and essay tests. If you want to improve your study skills, investigate the resources available on your campus. Many colleges and universities have study skills centers and learning resources centers that are staffed by professionals trained in study skills; other campuses use specially trained counselors, tutors, or advisors to serve this function. Often professors or teaching assistants are more than willing to help. Most of these services are free of charge to students, but you must seek them out.

Carol Mosher

When an instructor gives that famous assignment, "Read Chapter Eight for next time," what does she mean? There are two jobs for the student implicit in that assignment. The first is to understand; the second is to remember. The instructor does not care how the information is received or stored, just as long as it is.

Among several steps to understanding and remembering, the first is to be able to organize ideas into main ideas and details and then to see the relationships between and among these ideas. For instance, if you drive into a gas station and ask the mechanic to tell you what is wrong with your car, you would be unhappy if he said, "I can name all the parts of the carburetor, something I learned in my auto mechanics class." And yet, this is the kind of learning many students do, mistaking it for the real thing. The problem with our mechanic is that he has concentrated on the details, thinking that they are as important as the main ideas; maybe he is unable to tell the difference between the two. This kind of learning is insufficient and does not reflect the way experts in the field think. If you are to pass tests prepared by your instructors, who are experts in their fields, you need to learn to think like them.

One excellent way to organize your textbook study is to use the SQ4R study technique, with its six steps of Survey, Question, Read, Recite, Rite, and Review.

Survey

The purpose of the survey step is to aid understanding and increase reading speed. Research shows that students who survey before they read material read it 24 percent faster than do those who do not survey. Why? Because if you know where you are going, you get there faster.

How do you survey? Read the title. Think about it for a few seconds. What do you know about it already? What do you think the chapter will include? Next, read the introduction, which provides an overview of the chapter. Read all the headings and subheadings. Look at pictures, charts, or graphs. Read the summary; see how it mirrors the introduction. Finally, read any questions, terms, or other important material at the end of the chapter. This entire process should take not more than three to five minutes. Now return to the beginning of the chapter and start the second step.

Question

The question step helps reveal the organization of the chapter and the relationship of details to main ideas, so that you will not end up like our auto mechanic, not seeing the forest for the trees. To do the question step, simply change headings into questions. For example, if the heading is "racism," the obvious question is "What is racism?" Or if the subheading is "The Causes of Racism," the question would be "What are the causes of racism?" To begin relating ideas to each other, you can ask questions that relate subheadings to headings. If the heading is "Racism," and the subheading is "Forms of Discrimination," a good question would be "How does discrimination lead to racism?" or "Is discrimination a necessary part of racism?" Don't these sound like good test questions? You can discover questions in headings, from study guides, from class discussion, and throughout the text.

Read

Next, read to answer your questions. This reading is much different from simply starting at the beginning of every chapter and reading every word, hoping that important ideas somehow will pop into your brain. As you look at your textbook, it is easy to answer the question, "What are the causes of racism?" The answers may be numbered, appear in boldface type, or be the first sentence in each paragraph. A glance through your text will reveal how easy it is to understand the structure of a textbook. Nearly all textbooks are put together in a similar way, so once you understand this method, you can apply it to every text.

Recite

Once you have located the answer in the text, your next job is to put that information in short-term memory so that you will be able to retrieve it later. The recite step will accomplish that for you. How do you recite? Look at the question you have written, look away, and answer the question **out loud** and **in your own words**. Answering the question out loud helps you to remember the answer; answering in your own words ensures that you understand the answer.

If you are unable to answer the question or you do not understand it, mark it in your SQ4R notes so that you can listen especially for that point when it is discussed in class. You should do SQ4R with your chapter before you go to the class discussion on it. If you have not prepared for the class, you will be lost, trying to cope with new ideas, new vocabulary, and disorganization all at once.

When you have answered your question, simply move on to the next heading or subheading, make up a question, and answer it out loud and in your own words. Continue this process to the end of the chapter.

Rite

Rite, a phonetic rendering of "write," means you should learn to use cue notes. A cue is a word or phrase that helps you to recall longer phrases. For example, "soc." might represent "socialization" or some similar term that is too long to write out every time it is used. "Soc?" might represent "What is the definition of socialization?"

As you form the questions and find the answers, write them down in cue form. In this way, you can have all the questions and answers from your chapter in a brief format.

Review

The review step, the final task, is to ensure that what you have understood will be retrievable from your memory one, two, or several weeks after you study it. There are two important times to review. The first is before you finish a study session. Review what you have covered in that session by repeating the recite step. Ask yourself the question, look away, and answer it. If you cannot answer the question, look back at the answer, then ask yourself the question again. Repeat this process until you can answer the question.

The second review should take place once a week until you are tested on the material; again, use the recite process. This review should take no more than five to ten minutes.

SQ4R was formulated in the early 1940s. No one has discovered a better method for understanding and remembering textbook material. Research has demonstrated that use of SQ4R will ensure an average of 80 percent retention of textbook material. Many of you will do much better than that. Try it. The proof is in the performance.

Effective Test Taking

Most professors rely on periodic exams to assess students' knowledge of course material and determine final grades. Faithful study throughout the course is a necessary prerequisite for taking exams. Nevertheless, even the most well-prepared students often approach exams with some degree of anxiety and apprehension. Knowledge (and practice) of effective test-taking techniques can reduce some of this anxiety and increase the probability of receiving a high grade.

Exam questions typically fall into one of two categories: objective or subjective (essay) questions. Objective tests require short, specific answers. In contrast, subjective tests tend to require broader, in-depth answers. Objective questions typically do not rely on your instructor's personal judgment to determine whether or not they are correct. Subjective questions, however, are often graded on both form and content and depend, in part, on personal judgment to determine their quality. The answer to a subjective question may be technically correct yet not receive full credit if it does not provide enough information or is organized and written poorly.

Regardless of the type of test, certain strategies for preparing for and taking exams have proved effective. Although no technique can ensure success, research has shown that when the following practices are consistently followed they can be of great benefit to students.

Basic Strategies

Before the Exam: Preparation, of course, begins with basic study. If you have kept up with reading, class notes, and other assignments, preparation should be a matter of review rather than learning new material. These strategies are effective as the test draws near.

1. Take full advantage of any review time available from the instructor. Clear up any questions you may have about content and find out the exact structure of the test.
2. Review your SQ4R notes. Be alert to any problem areas.
3. Make up practice questions and answer them.
4. Use a "buddy" system. Compare your notes and practice questions with someone else in the class. You may have missed something that he or she noticed.
5. Get a good night's sleep the night before the test.
6. Bring all necessary materials and an extra pen and pencil.
7. Arrive at the testing center a few minutes early to obtain your favorite seat and get organized.

Once the Test Has Begun:

1. Read and follow all directions. Be alert to possible choices of which questions to answer, time limits, point values, and so on.
2. Quickly read through all the questions. Budget your time.
3. Answer the questions you are sure of first. Go back to the others.

On Completion:

1. Go back and check your answers.
2. Be certain you have not inadvertently omitted any questions and that you have followed the directions.
3. Check your spelling and grammar.

Objective Tests

Objective tests typically require short, specific answers testing your ability to recognize and recall information. Types of objective questions include multiple choice, matching, completion (fill-in-the-blanks), identification, and true/false.

When you take objective tests, it is especially important to follow specific directions since these exams are often scored by a computer or other device that has been programmed to accept only specific types of answers in specific places. By failing to use a pencil or making your pencil marks too light, for example, you can lose points even though your answer may be correct.

It is equally important to pay specific attention to point values of questions and sections. Objective tests often consist of a large number of questions that are worth only a few points each. Spending too much time on a question worth only two or three points can seriously jeopardize completion of the rest of the exam. It is better, in the long run, to miss a few points than run out of time and be forced to omit an entire section worth far more.

There are techniques for taking the various types of objective tests, which you should be able to learn at your campus learning center or other resource. You will find the information you gain worthwhile.

Subjective Tests

Subjective, or essay, questions are typically more general than objective questions and rely on your ability not only to recall or recognize information but also to synthesize, organize, and explain the information in depth. Because essay questions do tend to be broad, students often assume such questions require less study. In reality, however, they typically require more study because a deeper understanding of the material is required to answer the question successfully.

Many general test-taking strategies apply to subjective tests and should be followed. Reading and following directions is critical because students are often given a choice of questions to answer. Essay questions often contain specific directives indicating what to do and how to organize an answer. The following list includes some common directives and their meanings:

Analyze: break into parts
Choose: select
Comment: similar to "discuss"
Compare: show similarities or similarities and differences
Contrast: show differences
Compare and contrast: show similarities and differences
Criticize: examine the pro and con positions and give your judgment
Define: give the meaning
Discuss: give as much information as you can
Evaluate: make a judgment and include the reasons that led to this judgment
Explain: give reasons
Illustrate: give examples
Interrelate: show relationships among
List: make the major points stand out clearly
Show: explain
State: give the information
Trace: show step-by-step development

You should also be alert to key words such as **after**, **before**, and **briefly** and phrases such as **two out of three**, which specify and limit. By alerting yourself to these directives and key words, you can better organize your essay and avoid wasting time by providing information that is not required. The essay items in this study guide use several of these directives and key words. Note them as you use this guide and take essay exams.

Outline your answer before actually writing the essay to be certain you have included all the major points in logical order. If you run out of time, some instructors will give partial credit for material in outline form. Unless you are told differently, essays should be in paragraph form with a thesis sentence and a conclusion. Remember, many instructors also grade on spelling and punctuation, as well as on organization, so be certain your essay is grammatically correct. Your answer will also be enhanced if you use the correct terminology of your discipline.

I hope that you will find these techniques and strategies helpful. Learning and using proper study techniques will benefit you throughout your academic and professional career.

Essay Questions: Understanding Format

Margo Elliott

Often students complain that even though they studied their material diligently, they still did not do well on their exams. This is particularly true in the case of essay questions. Students may feel that the instructor asked the "wrong" questions or stated them in a confusing or ambiguous manner. This may be due in part to the way the information is learned and in part to how the information is understood. Memorizing facts, theories, and data is insufficient in answering questions that require anything more than simple knowledge. For facts to be useful, one must be able to understand and apply those facts, and this is what your instructors are testing.

Psychologists have suggested that there are different levels of comprehension and that these levels can be represented by a categorization scheme or taxonomy. One such system is Bloom's stage theory of cognitive development.[*] Bloom suggests that there are six stages of understanding, each stage becoming successively more difficult and requiring a higher level of comprehension.

Stage one is the knowledge level. Knowledge questions require simple memorization and recall of various terms, theories, and research.

Stage two is the comprehension level and involves the ability to understand nonliteral statements, such as examples, symbolism, and metaphors.

Stage three is the application level and requires the application of concepts or scientific terminology.

The fourth stage, analysis, uses the ability to recognize assumptions, to comprehend relationships, and to distinguish facts from hypotheses.

Stages five and six involve synthesis and evaluation, respectively. These levels generally require a greater knowledge base of the discipline than is typically required in an introductory course. These cognitive abilities would more likely be used in upper level and graduate work and will therefore not be discussed. To clarify further, let's use a fictitious example.

Animal specialists have developed two methods you can use to teach your dog not to bark at the letter carrier. The first method (A) involves verbal punishment and reprimand when your dog (Sadie) barks at the letter carrier. The second method (B) uses reward and verbal praise when Sadie does not bark at the letter carrier. After months of training, the specialists concluded that although both methods worked, method B was more effective than method A.

Assume that you have read a text that presented a detailed account of the preceding research. Here are sample questions your instructor might ask that reflect the various levels: Notice how a greater degree of understanding is reflected in the increasing complexity of the questions.

---

[*] Bloom, Benjamin S. *Cognitive Domain* (New York: McKay, 1969).

Level I: Knowledge
1. What is the dog's name?
2. How many methods of training were discussed?
(Note that these are simple recall of concrete and specific information.)

Level II: Comprehension
1. Explain the two methods of training.
2. Give examples of appropriate reward and punishment for Sadie.
(Note the slightly higher level skills involved in answering these questions. Be sure to understand that explain does not mean list.)

Level III: Application
1. Using either method A or method B, devise a training program for a dog that barks at the letter carrier.
2. How might these methods be used for training Sadie to shake hands?
(Note that these questions require applying an understanding of concepts and facts.)

Level IV: Analysis
1. Explain why method B is a more successful training program than method A.
2. Can these methods be generalized to child-rearing techniques? Be specific.
(Note that at this level individual thought is required.)

When preparing to study for exams, you will want to be alert to these various forms that content questions can take. It might also be helpful to ask your instructor if he or she would be willing to provide sample questions.

In the essay sections of each chapter you will find questions that reflect the various levels. You may wish to refer back to this section when preparing those questions.

CHAPTER ONE

Groups and Relationships: A Sociological Sampler

Overview

This chapter introduces the discipline of sociology: what it studies and how it differs from other social sciences. It opens with a discussion of the beginnings of sociology in the works of moral statisticians such as Quételet, Guerry, and Morselli. Special attention is paid to Durkheim's work in the area of suicide. It then discusses the main focus of sociology—the group—and distinguishes among types of groups. It introduces both micro and macro sociology. (The trend from micro to macro will be a major focus of this text.) It also discusses the scientific nature of sociology and highlights some of the challenges, drawbacks, and advantages of studying self-aware subjects. Chapter 1 offers some examples of research techniques such as unobtrusive measures and validation research designed to minimize potential problems. Stanley Milgram's "small world" research and MacKay's study of parallel networks are highlighted as the "over-the-shoulder" examples. (The "over-the-shoulder" items will be an essential feature of other chapters.) The chapter concludes with a brief discussion of the historical background of sociology and a discussion of the compatibility of the doctrine of free will and the social sciences.

Capsule Summary

Sociology began when **moral statisticians** such as **Quételet**, **Guerry**, and **Morselli** began to study suicide rates in Europe. Emile Durkheim further elaborated on these data and argued that high suicide rates reflect a **weakness in the web of relationships among members of a society**. Gradually the study of moral statistics began to uncover the **social causes of individual behavior**, and **sociology** was born.

Sociology shares with the other **social sciences** an interest in human behavior. It differs from the other social sciences in its primary focus: **the patterns and processes of human social relations**. The study of **group behavior** is thus of major concern to sociologists. Indeed, sociology is often divided into **micro** and **macro** sociology, depending on the size of the group studied.

Groups may be large or small, but they all share the common characteristic of **social relations among members**. The smallest possible group is the **dyad** or group of two. **Triads** (groups of three) are of particular interest to sociologists because they often demonstrate the rules of **transitivity** and **coalition formation**. The patterns of social relations among members of a group are termed **networks**. **Sociograms** are used to study the structure of networks. Groups vary not only in size but also in the degree of intimacy shared by members. Groups in which the members share a good deal of intimacy are termed **primary groups**; those in which relationships are more impersonal are termed **secondary groups**.

Science is a method of discovery. **Science** uses **theories**, very general statements about how some portion of the world fits together and functions. Social scientists are in a unique position among scientists because their subjects are self-aware. **Unobtrusive measures** provide an interesting technique employed to test the accuracy of data. Although bias does present a potential problem in sociological research, the nature of scientific inquiry minimizes this bias. Science often seeks to challenge previous assumptions and theories.

Mass society theorists were concerned that **modernization** had led to a breakdown in social relationships among urban dwellers. (The theme of modernization will be dealt with extensively in later chapters.) Milgram's "small world" research and MacKay's study of **parallel networks** challenged many of these assumptions.

The origins of the social sciences can be traced to philosophy, but it was not until recently that research was conducted in the social sciences. Economist **Adam Smith** (1776) may be considered the first real social scientist. **Auguste Comte** used the term **sociology** in the 1830s, and early European sociologists included **Spenser, Tönnies**, and **Durkheim**. **Albion Small** and **W. E. B. DuBois** were important in the development of sociology in **America**.

The doctrine of **free will** is compatible with the social sciences even though on the surface it may appear contradictory. All social science theories assume that humans possess the ability to reason and make choices. These choices are, however, predictable since people will choose what they find rewarding given their circumstances, information, and preferences.

Key Concepts

You should be able to explain the concepts in the following list. You should also be able to cite several examples of each concept. The page number after each concept indicates where the concept is introduced.

Key Research Studies

Be familiar with both the methodology and the results of the research studies cited here.
   Durkheim: *Suicide*—study of suicide rates based on Morselli's data 5
   Bainbridge and Stark: use of unobtrusive measures in studying geographical patterns in
      metaphysical beliefs and practices 15
   Hirschi: delinquency study using validation research 17
   Milgram: "small world" research networks 20
   J. Ross MacKay: parallel social networks in Canada 22

Key Figures

You should be able to associate each person with his contribution.
   André Michel Guerry: co-founder of moral statistics
   Adolphe Quételet: co-founder of moral statistics
   Henry Morselli: gathered statistics on suicide
   Emile Durkheim: wrote *Suicide* and argued that high suicide rates reflect a weakness in
      social relationships
   Charles H. Cooley: coined the term *primary group*
   Adam Smith: economist and first social scientist
   Auguste Comte: coined the term *sociology*
   Herbert Spenser: published *Principles of Sociology*
   Ferdinand Tönnies: published *Gemeinschaft and Gesellschaft*
   Albion Small: founded first sociology department in America at the University of
      Chicago
   W. E. B. DuBois: created a sociological laboratory and directed the Atlanta University
      Conferences

Key Theories

Be prepared to explain the assumptions of these theories and, when applicable, to cite
related research findings.
   Micro sociology
   Macro sociology
   Free will

Completion

Although each statement has only one blank, some may require two or more words for completion.

1. The co-founders of moral statistics were _____ and _____.

2. Durkheim argued that _____ suicide rates reflect weaknesses in the web of relationships among members of society.

3. The topic of sociology is _____.

4. _____ sociologists tend to focus on large groups and whole societies.

5. The smallest social group is a _____.

6. "Any friend of yours is a friend of mine" demonstrates the rule of _____.

7. The ability to get one's way over the opposition of others is termed _____.

8. The patterns of relationships among members of a group are often called _____.

9. _____ groups are characterized by great intimacy among members.

10. _____ measures obtain information without disturbing the objects of the research.

11. Comparison of results when different measures are used is one way to assess the _____ of sociological data.

12. Milgram and MacKay both studied the existence of _____.

13. MacKay discovered that language barriers within Canada are much _____ than are national boundaries.

14. The essence of the scientific method is _____.

15. The proper approach to research is to try to _____ those things that the researcher actually believes to be true.

16. Personal bias is possibly a more serious problem in _____ than for natural or physical sciences.

17. Scientific explanations must take the form of theories, and these must be the object of testing by _____.

18. The term *sociology* was first suggested by _____.

19. _____ created a sociological laboratory and directed the Altanta University Conferences.

20. The doctrine of _____ argues that humans possess the capacity for choosing among alternatives and, therefore, can be held responsible for the choices they make.

Multiple Choice

1. Nineteenth-century statistics comparing suicide rates from one nation to another showed that:
    a. the rates were extremely stable year to year
    b. the rates varied little from one nation to another
    c. during the nineteenth century the rates declined sharply
    d. all of the above
    e. none of the above

2. Emile Durkheim argued that:
    a. traditional rural societies were deficient in the kinds of warm interpersonal relationships typical of modern societies
    b. high suicide rates reflect a weakness in an individual's personality
    c. high suicide rates reflect weaknesses in the web of relationships among members of society
    d. a and c
    e. a and b

3. Sociologists differ from psychologists in that psychologists have typically studied:
    a. industrial societies
    b. illegal behavior
    c. preliterate societies
    d. political organization
    e. individual behavior

4. The primary subject of sociology is:
    a. the individual
    b. the group
    c. preliterate societies
    d. illegal behavior
    e. political organization

5. The *main* difference between micro sociology and macro sociology is:
   a. the size of the group studied
   b. the research method used
   c. the training of the researcher
   d. the degree of industrialization achieved by the group studied
   e. the presence of self-aware subjects in micro sociology

6. The social sciences include:
   a. anthropology
   b. political science
   c. sociology
   d. a and c
   e. all of the above

7. Intransitive triads:
   a. are demonstrated by the statement "any friend of yours is a friend of mine"
   b. are unstable and usually break up
   c. may lead to coalition formation—two against one
   d. all of the above
   e. b and c

8. A triad is:
   a. a group of three
   b. the smallest sociological group
   c. always intransitive and unstable
   d. all of the above
   e. a and c

9. Primary group members:
   a. share a good deal of intimacy with each other
   b. gain much of their self-esteem from their groups
   c. often refer to themselves as "we"
   d. a and c
   e. all of the above

10. Which of the following would most likely *not* be considered a primary group?
    a. a political party
    b. a group of intimate friends
    c. a family
    d. b and c
    e. none of the above

11. When researchers test data against some independent standard of accuracy, they are:
    a. using an unobtrusive measure
    b. conducting validation research
    c. using self-reports
    d. a and c
    e. none of the above

12. In his study of delinquency, Travis Hirschi:
    a. used self-reports
    b. conducted validation research
    c. used both interviews and questionnaires
    d. a and b
    e. all of the above

13. Milgram's "small world" research:
    a. contributed considerable support to mass society theories
    b. found that most of the letters did not reach their designated receiver
    c. discovered that people throughout the country were united by "chains of attachment"
    d. discovered a very strong interest in astrology in the Far West
    e. a and b

14. The researcher who arranged to have auto mechanics note the position of the radio dials in cars they serviced in order to ascertain what stations people listened to while driving used:
    a. an unobtrusive measure
    b. validation research
    c. self-reported behavior studies
    d. b and c
    e. all of the above

15. The term *sociology* was first suggested by:
    a. Adolphe Quételet
    b. Auguste Comte
    c. Emile Durkheim
    d. Charles H. Cooley
    e. Albion Small

16. Which of the following early sociologists is *not* correctly paired with his contribution?
    a. Ferdinand Tönnies: published *Gemeinschaft and Gesellschaft*
    b. Emile Durkheim: suggested the term *sociology*
    c. Albion Small: founder of the first sociology department in North America
    d. a and b
    e. b and c

17. The author considers the field of sociology to be about _____ years old.
    a. 2,000
    b. 300
    c. 200
    d. 100
    e. 20

18. Reasons for the existence of parallel networks include:
    a. racism
    b. language
    c. distance
    d. a and b
    e. all of the above

19. Which of the following statements is/are true?
    a. the essence of the scientific method is systematic skepticism
    b. the purpose of scientific research is to test what we believe about the world
    c. because bias is a problem in sociological research, sociologists must completely rid themselves of personal biases before beginning research
    d. a and b
    e. all of the above

20. The doctrine of free will:
    a. is incompatible with the social sciences
    b. assumes that humans have the ability to reason and to make choices
    c. assumes that people will seek those things they find rewarding and will avoid those they find unrewarding
    d. b and c
    e. all of the above

Essay

In each chapter Questions 1 and 2 are designed to reflect the cognitive levels described in the Introduction. In each case the general topic in question is divided into three smaller questions, each requiring a different level of understanding. Some questions tap the levels of knowledge, comprehension, and application, and others tap comprehension, application, and analyses. The level is indicated in parentheses. You might wish to refer back to the Introduction for a more detailed explanation of the cognitive level in question. Admittedly, some of these essays are fairly long and difficult, but by using them for practice you should be able to test yourself on how well you have mastered the material in question.

1. A. Name some research techniques used to study self-aware subjects. (knowledge)
    B. Explain these research techniques. (comprehension)
    C. Design a simple study that uses one of the above techniques. (application)

2. A. Name some assumptions of mass society theorists. (knowledge)
   B. Explain Milgram's research. (comprehension)
   C. Show how Milgram's results did or did not support mass society theory. (analysis)

3. Trace the development of the social sciences from their origins in philosophy to the present.

4. Discuss the principles of transitivity and coalition formation. Explain how the study of networks is relevant to both micro and macro sociology.

5. Explain the following statement: "It is only because people's choices are predictable that it is possible to claim that they have free will."

Answers

Completion

1. Adolphe Quételet and André Guerry
2. high
3. interpersonal relationships (or groups)
4. macro
5. dyad
6. transitivity
7. power
8. social networks
9. primary
10. unobtrusive
11. validity
12. social networks
13. less powerful
14. systematic skepticism
15. disprove
16. social
17. systematic research
18. Auguste Comte
19. W. E. B. DuBois
20. free will

Multiple Choice

1. a
2. c
3. e
4. b
5. a
6. e
7. e
8. a
9. e
10. a
11. b
12. e
13. c
14. a
15. b
16. b
17. d
18. e
19. d
20. d

CHAPTER TWO

Concepts for Social and Cultural Theories

Overview

Part I opens with a discussion of the eight steps in *theory construction* and *theory testing* and the importance of concepts and theories in science. Chapter 2 begins with a discussion of two important concepts in sociology: society and culture. Patterns of intergroup relations are discussed; social stratification is introduced; and the concepts of class, mobility, achieved status, and ascribed status are explained. Cultural components such as norms, values, and roles are discussed. Cultural and social theories of assimilation are then illustrated through the works of Zborowski and Herzog, Covello, and Steinberg. The chapter closes with a look at the importance of reference groups.

Capsule Summary

Scientific **theories** exist to explain why. **Theories** are **general** in that they apply to all instances and make predictions that can be checked out. The scientific process includes both **theory construction** and **theory testing**. A sociologist engaged in theory construction and testing would first begin by **wondering** and then proceed to **conceptualize**, **theorize**, **operationalize**, **hypothesize**, **observe**, **analyze**, and, lastly, **assess**. **Concepts** are used in science to classify things that are alike. They are abstract and serve as the building blocks for **theories**. **Theories** are statements that say why and how several concepts are related. Theories are general, whereas **hypotheses** tell the implications of predictions in specific situations.

    Society and **culture** are essential concepts in sociology. A **society** is a group of people characterized by social relationships, relative self-sufficiency and independence, duration over time, a physical location, and a common **culture**. **Culture**, on the other hand, is the pattern of living that people have developed and handed down through generations. **Norms**, **values**, and **roles** are important components of culture. **Norms** refer to rules or guidelines for behavior, and **values** serve as standards for assessing the desirability or undesirability of something; **norms** and **values** are often related. **Roles** refer to collections of norms associated with particular positions in society. Cultures differ not only in their actual **norms**, **values**, and **roles** but also in the relative importance attached to them.

    Social stratification refers to the unequal distribution of rewards among members of a society. Societies are "layered," and these layers constitute **classes**: groups of people sharing a similar position (or status) in a society. Movement within a stratification system is termed **mobility**, and the direction it takes may be **upward** or **downward**. Position (status) within the stratification system may be based on either **achievement** or **ascription**.

    Whenever members of one culture immigrate to another, different patterns of intergroup relations may occur. If the immigrant group gives up its old culture and totally adopts the new, **assimilation** has occurred. If members of the new culture resist full acceptance of the immigrant group, then **prejudice** and **discrimination** against the immigrant group may result. In such cases, the immigrant group may become a **subordinate group** in the new culture. In other cases, **accommodation** may occur, which results in **cultural pluralism**. Often the immigrant group becomes a **subculture** within the new culture.

During the nineteenth and twentieth centuries many immigrant groups were the objects of **prejudice** and **discrimination** when they arrived in the United States and Canada. The experiences of both Jewish and Italian immigrants in the United States provide interesting examples of cultural differences. **Zborowski** and **Herzog** studied **shtetl** life in Europe to gain information on the cultural background of Jewish immigrants. They concluded that this background was a major factor in facilitating **upward mobility** after immigration. **Steinberg** further investigated this area and found that the **occupational background** of Jewish immigrants also facilitated upward mobility, thus implying a more social rather than cultural explanation. In his study of Italian immigrants, Covello found that their cultural background initially served as a deterrent to upward mobility. Their **reference group** identification probably was also a factor because most Italian immigrants considered their **reference group** to be those who remained in Italy. Thus, the research studies indicate that differences in cultural background may partly explain the differing rates of initial upward mobility between Jewish and Italian immigrants. Recent data indicate that prejudice against Jews (**anti-Semitism**) and Italians in the United States and Canada seems to have diminished markedly as a result of **assimilation** (particularly intermarriage) and **accommodation**.

Key Concepts

You should be able to explain the concepts listed here, as well as be able to cite several examples of each concept.

Key Research Studies

You should be familiar with both the methodology and the results of the following research studies.

Glock and Stark, Stark and others: anti-Semitism in the United States 50
Zborowski and Herzog: cultural backgrounds of Jewish immigrants 52
Covello: cultural background of Italian immigrants 54
Steinberg: cultural and occupational backgrounds of Jewish immigrants 57

Key Theories

Eight steps in theory construction and theory testing
Cultural theory
Social theory

Completion

1. _____ are abstractions that are used to classify sets of things that are alike.

2. A(n) _____ is a group of people who are united by special relations; it is relatively self-sufficient and independent.

3. _____ is the complex pattern of living that humans have developed and pass from generation to generation.

4. _____ are statements that say why and how several concepts are related.

5. A _____ tells us the implications of a prediction in the specific situation we observe.

6. Stratification is the _____ distribution of rewards among members of a society.

7. When a lawyer's daughter becomes a factory worker, we can say she has experienced _____ mobility.

8. _____ statuses are derived from inheritance, whereas _____ statuses are derived from individual merit.

9. _____ refers to negative attitudes toward a group, and _____ refers to actions taken against a group.

10. Norms are _____ governing behavior.

11. The _____ of a culture identify its ideals.

12. A(n) _____ is a collection of norms associated with a particular position in a society.

13. The process of exchanging one culture for another is termed _____.

14. _____ occurs when accommodation results in the continued existence of several distinctive cultures within a society.

15. A distinctive set of beliefs, morals, customs, and the like developed or maintained by a group within a larger society is called a(n) _____.

16. Prejudice against Jews is termed _____.

17. Marrying someone of another ethnic background is called _____.

18. Zborowski and Herzog found that the cultural background of Jews stressed _____ as an important value.

19. Covello found that the cultural background of Italian immigrants did not serve to foster their achievement of _____.

20. Groups that individuals identify with and whose norms and values serve as their basis for self-judgment are termed _____.

Multiple Choice

1. Which of the following statements is/are true?
   a. concepts are names used to identify some set or class of things that are said to be alike
   b. scientific concepts are concrete; they identify things, not ideas
   c. concepts are the building blocks of any science
   d. a and c
   e. all of the above

2. Scientific theories:
   a. are specific in nature
   b. must include or imply some conclusions that can be empirically verified by direct physical observation
   c. are more specific than hypotheses
   d. a and b
   e. all of the above

3. Which of the following are the *last* three steps in the scientific process?
   a. observation, analysis, and assessment
   b. operationalization, observation, and analysis
   c. observation, conceptualization, and analysis
   d. conceptualization, analysis, and assessment
   e. none of the above

4. Characteristics of societies include:
   a. a definite physical location
   b. relative self-sufficiency and independence
   c. existence over time
   d. a and c
   e. all of the above

5. Culture is:
   a. everything that humans learn
   b. a group of people united by social relationships
   c. often synonymous with nation
   d. a and c
   e. all of the above

6. When a factory worker's child becomes a physician we say that he or she has experienced:
   a. upward mobility
   b. downward mobility
   c. circular mobility
   d. horizontal mobility
   e. none of the above

7. Ascribed statuses may be based on:
   a. family background
   b. individual merit
   c. genetic inheritance
   d. a and c
   e. all of the above

8. The caste system in India:
   a. is an extreme example of a stratification system based on achieved status
   b. is based on an individual's ability to merit
   c. is an extreme example of a stratification system based on ascribed status
   d. a and b
   e. all of the above

9. Rules governing behavior are termed _____.
   a. values
   b. beliefs
   c. norms
   d. roles
   e. none of the above

10. Which of the following statements is/are true?
    a. the values of a culture identify its ideals
    b. norms are quite general, whereas values are specific
    c. values justify the norms
    d. a and c
    e. all of the above

11. _____ refers to negative attitudes toward a group, and _____ refers to negative actions against a group.
    a. prejudice, discrimination
    b. discrimination, prejudice
    c. subordination, discrimination
    d. prejudice, assimilation

12. Which of the following statements is/are true?
    a. social life is structured by roles
    b. cultures differ in their evaluation of various roles
    c. some roles are thought to be more demanding than others
    d. b and c
    e. all of the above

13. The process of exchanging one culture for another is termed:
    a. assimilation
    b. accommodation
    c. cultural pluralism
    d. discrimination
    e. cultural exchange

14. The existence of different religions side by side in the United States today is an example of:
    a. cultural pluralism
    b. assimilation
    c. subordinate groups
    d. discrimination
    e. cultural lag

15. Anti-Semitism refers to prejudice against _____.
    a. Italians
    b. blacks
    c. Jews
    d. Roman Catholics
    e. none of the above

16. According to Covello, immigrants from Southern Italy brought with them to America:
    a. a "cult of scholarship" and emphasis on learning
    b. the belief that school was harmful and a threat to family loyalty
    c. extensive training in the professional and middle-class occupations
    d. a and c
    e. none of the above

17. Steinberg found that many of the immigrant Jews:
    a. had been farmers and hence could find employment only in unskilled occupations
    b. were trained in skilled and professional occupations
    c. were single men who planned to return to their families in Europe
    d. a and c
    e. none of the above

18. In contrast to Jewish immigrants, Italian immigrants:
    a. rapidly achieved upward mobility
    b. rapidly learned English and assimilated into American culture
    c. came with their families and planned to stay in America
    d. all of the above
    e. none of the above

19. Studies by Stark and others on anti-Semitism found that by the middle and late 1960s:
    a. prejudice against Jews was increasing
    b. prejudice against Jews had declined greatly
    c. prejudice against Italians had declined
    d. prejudice against Italians had increased
    e. none of the above

20. Reference groups:
    a. are groups that individuals identify with
    b. are the people whose approval counts most with us
    c. must be present to influence a person's behavior
    d. a and b
    e. all of the above

Essay

1. A. Describe the research findings of Zborowski and Herzog and of Steinberg. (knowledge)
    B. Do you feel the cultural backgrounds of other minorities have influenced their mobility? Give specific examples. (comprehension)
    C. Contrast the cultural backgrounds of Jewish and Italian immigrants, and show how these backgrounds influenced their mobility. (analysis)

2. A. Briefly explain the terms *norm, value,* and *role.* (knowledge)
    B. Give two examples of the preceding terms. (comprehension)
    C. Interrelate these concepts using specific examples. (analysis)

3. Discuss some of the characteristics and uses of scientific concepts.

4. Distinguish between society and culture, and discuss the characteristics of each.

5. Discuss some patterns of intergroup relations that might occur when immigrant groups arrive in a new culture. Give examples from American history.

Answers

Completion
1. concepts
2. society
3. culture
4. theories
5. hypothesis
6. unequal
7. downward
8. ascribed, achieved
9. prejudice, discrimination
10. rules
11. values
12. role
13. assimilation
14. cultural pluralism
15. subculture
16. anti-Semitism
17. intermarriage
18. education
19. upward mobility
20. reference groups

Multiple Choice
1. d
2. b
3. a
4. e
5. a
6. a
7. d
8. c
9. c
10. d
11. a
12. e
13. a
14. a
15. c
16. b
17. b
18. e
19. b
20. d

CHAPTER THREE

Micro Sociology: Testing Interaction Theories

Overview

Chapter 3 opens with a discussion of scientific theories of micro sociology, such as rational choice theory, exchange theory, and symbolic interactionism. Cooley and Mead's works on socialization and the development of the self are explained. The importance of attachments is introduced and discussed in this chapter. (This theme will be developed throughout the text.) The chapter then discusses research, with emphasis on the importance of ascertaining causation. Techniques for determining causation are described. Ofshe's experimental study of attachments and conformity is highlighted as the "over-the-shoulder" example. The author's study with Lofland on attachments and conversion is keynoted as an example of nonexperimental research. A discussion of replication concludes the chapter.

Capsule Summary

Rational choice theory, exchange theory, and **symbolic interaction** are examples of **micro theories** in sociology. Micro theories assume that people make choices based on **rewards** and **costs**. **Rational choice theories** assume that since rewards are typically obtained from others, people engage in **exchange relationships** and over time tend to establish **stable exchange partnerships** with others. **Attachments** emerge from such relationships, and **norms** function to ensure some basis for predictability. **Symbolic interaction** focuses on the importance of **symbols**, which stand for or indicate other things. Symbols are essential for human communication. **Cooley** and **Mead**, founders of symbolic interaction, focused on the processes of **socialization** and the development of the **self**.

    Research is the process of making systematic observations. Much research focuses on testing specific **hypotheses**. Research tries to establish **causation** by establishing the presence of the three criteria of **causation: correlation, time order**, and **nonspuriousness**. **Correlation** can be established if it can be shown that two things vary or change in unison. **Time order** can be demonstrated if it can be shown that the cause (often termed the **independent variable**) precedes the effect (often termed the **dependent variable**). **Nonspuriousness** can be established if it can be shown that the effect was not produced by something else. Typically research studies are **replicated** by others to determine whether or not the same results are consistently obtained.

    Sociological research may be either **experimental** or **nonexperimental**. Nonexperimental research is probably more common since many of the problems typically studied by sociologists do not lend themselves well to laboratory research. Experiments offer greater control over the subjects. Nonexperimental research findings are more subject to risk. **Ofshe's** study of **attachments** and **conformity** is an example of experimental research. He was able to demonstrate **causation** by establishing the three criteria. He used **controls** and **randomization** to rule out the possibility of **spuriousness** and employed a **test of significance** to rule out chance. **Stark and Lofland's** study of attachments and conversion is an interesting example of nonexperimental research. They too were able to establish **correlation** and **time order** but, as is often the case with **observational studies, nonspuriousness** was more difficult to ascertain.

Key Concepts

You should be able to explain the following concepts. You should also be able to cite several examples of each concept.

Micro sociology 70	Attachment 76
Rational choice proposition 71	Causation 78
Altruism 72	Correlation (positive and negative) 79
Reward 73	Nonspuriousness 79
Cost 73	Variable 82
Exchange relations 73	Independent variable 82
Goods 73	Dependent variable 82
Social interaction 73	Experimental control 82
Symbol 73	Randomization 82
Self 74	Test of significance 83
Socialization 74	Nonexperimental research 84
"Looking glass self" 74	Field observation 85
Mind (Mead) 74	Replication 87
"Taking the role of the other" 74	

Key Research Studies

You should be familiar with both the methodology and the results of the research studies cited here.

Dion: influence of appearance on perception of children's misbehavior 68

Ofshe: study of attachments and conformity among college students (experimental study) 80

Stark and Lofland: nonexperimental research on conformity and conversion 84

Key Figures

You should be able to associate each person with his contribution and explain any concepts or theories associated with him.

Charles H. Cooley: co-founder of symbolic interactionism; "looking glass self"; socialization and development of the self

George Herbert Mead: co-founder of symbolic interactionism; "taking the role of the other"; mind and self

Key Theories

Be prepared to explain the assumptions of these theories and, when applicable, to cite related research findings.

Micro sociology theories (in general)
Rational choice theories
Symbolic interactionism
Exchange theory
"Looking glass self"

Completion

1. When a theory pertains to the behavior of individuals or small groups it is in the realm of _____ sociology.

2. All micro theories in the social sciences assert that _____ is the most basic aspect of human behavior.

3. The more formal variety of interaction theories in sociology are referred to as _____ theories, whereas the less formal, older variety are referred to as _____ theories.

4. Social science proceeds on the principle that, given our options and preferences, we choose to do that which we can expect to be most _____.

5. Psychologists believe behavior is shaped by _____.

6. Humans seek what they perceive to be _____ and avoid what they perceive to be _____.

7. Unselfish behavior to benefit others is termed _____ .

8. _____ is the process by which we influence one another.

9. _____ are things that stand for or indicate other things and are of primary importance to the theory of _____.

10. Both Cooley and Mead concluded that each person's sense of self is _____.

11. Mead used the concept of _____ to identify understanding of symbols and _____ to identify our learned understanding of the responses of others.

12. Mead termed the ability to put ourselves in another's place the ability to _____.

13. Over time people tend to establish stable _____ partnerships.

14. A stable and persistent pattern of interaction between two people is termed a(n) _____.

15. _____ is the process of making systematic observations.

16. _____ are specific predictions about the empirical or observable world.

17. The three criteria of causation are _____, _____, and _____.

18. The independant variable is used to indicate a(n) _____, and the dependent variable is used to indicate a(n) _____.

19. Ofshe found a significant correlation between _____ and conformity among students.

20. Stark and Lofland's study of _____ and conversion is an example of _____ research.

Multiple Choice

1. Which of the following statements is/are true?
    a. all micro theories in the social sciences assert that choice is the most basic aspect of human behavior
    b. sociologists differ from economists in that economists greatly expand the concepts of rewards and costs
    c. exchange theory is an example of a macro sociology theory
    d. a and b
    e. none of the above

2. Rational choice theories include:
    a. symbolic interaction theory
    b. conflict theory
    c. exchange theory
    d. a and c
    e. all of the above

3. Micro sociology departs from the other micro social science theories in that micro sociology:
    a. expands the concepts of reward and cost
    b. recognizes that much of what we want can only be gotten from others
    c. defines goods as the whole range of rewards that people seek
    d. a and b
    e. all of the above

4. Micro sociology consists primarily of the study of:
   a. individuals
   b. face-to-face interaction in small groups
   c. explaining the regularities and patterns that arise out of interaction and exchanges
   d. b and c
   e. none of the above

5. Symbols:
   a. are things that stand for or indicate other things
   b. are important for human communication
   c. are part of our genetic make-up
   d. a and b
   e. all of the above

6. The "looking glass self" is associated with:
   a. Charles H. Cooley
   b. George H. Mead
   c. Richard Ofshe
   d. John Lofland
   e. George Homans

7. Mead considered the mind to be:
   a. our learned understanding of the responses of others to our conduct
   b. our understanding of symbols
   c. an innate component of the brain
   d. all of the above
   e. none of the above

8. Mead argued that a child cannot take an effective part in most games until he or she:
   a. can take the role of the other
   b. has developed a superego
   c. has developed a sense of self
   d. a and c
   e. all of the above

9. Stable exchange partnerships:
   a. are of special importance to us
   b. are restricted to goods and services
   c. often lead to the forming of attachments
   d. a and c
   e. all of the above

10. Specific predictions about the empirical or observable world are termed:
   a. theories
   b. variables
   c. controls
   d. hypotheses
   e. norms

11. Criteria for establishing causality include:
   a. replication, time order, and correlation
   b. correlation, time order, and spuriousness
   c. correlation, nonspuriousness, and time order
   d. correlation, spuriousness, and time order
   e. correlation, time order, and replication

12. _____ occurs when two factors appear correlated with one seeming to cause the other, when, in reality, the correlation is caused by a third, unnoticed factor.
   a. nonspuriousness
   b. spuriousness
   c. a negative correlation
   d. an inverse correlation
   e. none of the above

13. A positive correlation exists when:
   a. both factors decline
   b. both factors increase
   c. one factor rises while the other declines
   d. no relationship exists between the factors
   e. a and b

14. The term _____ variable is used to indicate a cause.
   a. dependent
   b. independent
   c. intervening
   d. spurious
   e. none of the above

15. To determine the criteria of nonspuriousness, Ofshe used:
   a. replication
   b. randomization
   c. controls
   d. b and c
   e. all of the above

16. In determining significance, both _____ and _____ are taken into account.
    a. number of subjects, size of the correlation
    b. number of subjects, time order of the experiment
    c. size of the correlation, time order of the experiment
    d. number of subjects, ages of the subjects
    e. none of the above

17. Stark and Lofland's study is an example of _____.
    a. field observation research
    b. the experimental method
    c. replication research
    d. secondary research
    e. all of the above

18. Stark and Lofland concluded that the primary basis for conversion to the Unification Church was:
    a. ideology
    b. brainwashing
    c. social class membership
    d. attachments
    e. a and b above

19. Replication studies of religious conversion have found:
    a. it is impossible to replicate nonexperimental research
    b. little support for the findings of Stark and Lofland's earlier study
    c. ideology rather than attachments plays the major role in determining conversion
    d. attachments play the major role in determining conversion
    e. b and c above

20. _____ is the most common form of symbolic interaction.
    a. gestures
    b. conversation
    c. body language
    d. reading
    e. writing

Essay

1. A. Name the three criteria of causation. (knowledge)
    B. Explain the three criteria of causation. (comprehension)
    C. Show how Ofshe was able to determine causation in his experiment. (analysis)

2. A. Define experimental and nonexperimental research. (knowledge)
    B. Design a study using either experimental or nonexperimental research. (application)
    C. Using examples from the text *compare and contrast* experimental and nonexperimental research. (analysis)

3. Distinguish between a theory and a hypothesis. Explain the following statement: "Researchers do not contribute to scientific progress by seeking evidence that will support theories but by doing their utmost to disprove them."

4. The premise that people make choices is central to micro theories in social science. Explain how this premise is incorporated by micro sociology.

5. Briefly explain symbolic interaction. Explain the theories of Cooley and Mead on the development of the self.

Answers

Completion
1. micro
2. choice
3. exchange, symbolic interaction
4. rewarding
5. reinforcement
6. rewards, costs
7. altruism
8. social interaction
9. symbols, symbolic-interactionism
10. socially created
11. mind, self
12. take the role of the other
13. exchange
14. attachment
15. research
16. hypotheses
17. correlation, time order, nonspuriousness
18. cause, effect
19. attachments
20. attachments, nonexperimental

Multiple Choice
1. a
2. d
3. e
4. d
5. d
6. a
7. b
8. d
9. d
10. d
11. c
12. b
13. e
14. b
15. d
16. a
17. a
18. d
19. d
20. b

CHAPTER FOUR

Macro Sociology: Testing Structural Theories

Overview

This chapter opens with examples of research on bystander apathy and of the relationship between religion and delinquency that illustrate the relationship between micro and macro sociology. The importance of attachments (a major theme of this text) is again emphasized. It then describes survey research and continues with a discussion of the elements of systems and the subject matter of macro sociology. Chapter 4 discusses *in depth* the three theories of macro sociology: functionalism, social evolution, and conflict. It closes with an "over-the shoulder" view of Paige's cross-cultural study of family structures and political conflict. Included at the end of this chapter is a special topic devoted to sampling.

Capsule Summary

Macro sociology is concerned with the study of **social structures: groups, institutions, organizations,** and **societies.** Micro and macro sociology are related, and often research in one area may overlap into the other. In their studies of **delinquency** and **religious commitment,** for example, **Hirschi** and **Stark** and **others** began by examining areas typically associated with micro sociology only to discover it was necessary instead to focus on areas in the realm of macro sociology.

Theories of **macro sociology** attempt to explain the existence of **social structures** and their **origins, differences,** and **interrelationships,** as well as the **interplay between the individual and the social structure.** Macro sociology views societies as social systems characterized by **separate structures, interdependency,** and **equilibrium.** Macro sociology often studies **institutions** and **classes. Institutions** are "clusters of roles, groups, organizations, customs, and activities that meet the basic needs of a society." Every society has at least **five basic institutions:** the **family,** the **economy, religion,** the **political order,** and **education. Classes** are groups of people who share a similar position in a society's stratification system. Macro sociology thus focuses on **institutions** and **classes** not only as separate structures but also as interrelated parts striving toward **equilibrium.**

Macro sociological theories include **functionalism, social evolution,** and **conflict theory.** Each of these focuses on **social structures,** yet each emphasizes different aspects of these structures and makes different assumptions about them.

Functionalism is concerned with **functions** or the part that each element of the system contributes to the whole. Functional theories have three components: They identify and explain an aspect of the system, that aspect's existence in terms of how it preserves another part from disruption, and the source of potential disruption. **Functionalism** also focuses on **functional alternatives** and **dysfunctions.**

Social evolution theories focus on the **development of social structures** over time and how they **adapt** to their **physical** and **social environment**. It postulates that those societies that have developed structures that enable them to adapt to their environment tend to grow and become more powerful and complex. It focuses on all societies and does not make value judgments regarding the direction of change.

Conflict theory considers **conflicts within a structure** that arise from the **differing interests of competitive groups**. It emphasizes how the structure may be shaped by the interests of these groups, especially the more **powerful** ones who serve their needs at the expense of the less powerful. **Marx** argued that the social structures are created by the **ruling class**. **Weber** expanded the concept and emphasized the importance of **status groups**.

Macro sociology often uses **survey research**. **Samples** are drawn and **questionnaires** or **interviews** are administered. Attention is payed to ensuring that the criteria of causality are met. (The studies of both Paige and Stark and others illustrate this.) Although macro sociology typically focuses on groups, institutions, and organizations, occasionally whole societies are compared and contrasted. **Paige's** research on **kinship structure** and **political conflict** used such a cross-cultural comparison and is an example of research in **macro sociology**.

Key Concepts

Be prepared to explain the concepts listed here and to cite several examples of each concept.

The following concepts are contained in Special Topic 1.

Key Research Studies

You should be familiar with both the methodology and the results of the following research studies.

Darley and Latenè: bystander apathy 90

Hirschi and Stark: delinquency and religious commitment 92

Stark and others: church membership, geographical area, and delinquency 96

Paige: comparative study of family systems of primitive societies 105

Key Figures

Be able to associate each person with his contribution and explain any concepts or theories associated with him.

Karl Marx: conflict theory; "the ruling class"

Max Weber: status group

Gerhard Lenski: social evolution

Key Theories

You should be able to explain the assumptions of the theories and, when applicable, cite related research findings.

Macro sociology theories (in general)

Functionalism

Social evolution

Conflict theory

Completion

1. The results of the research by Darley and Latenè found that the larger the group believed to be present, the _____ an individual will feel personal responsibility to act in an emergency.

2. In _____ the data are collected by personal interview or questionnaire.

3. A relationship is _____ if it disappears when some third variable is controlled.

4. Macro sociological theories attempt to explain the existence of _____.

5. _____ sociologists assume societies are systems.

6. Because the parts of a system are interdependent, they tend to fall into some kind of _____ or balance.

7. The five basic institutions in any society include religion, the political order, _____, _____, and _____.

8. _____ are clusters of specialized roles, groups, organizations, customs, and activities devoted to meeting social _____.

9. One adult couple and their children constitute a _____ family.

10. Another structure by which the same function can be accomplished is termed a _____.

11. Arrangements among structures that harm or distort the system are termed _____.

12. _____ theories suggest that societies with structures that enable them to adapt to their physical and social environments have a better chance for survival than do societies that fail to develop such structures.

13. A faulty assumption made by nineteenth-century social evolutionists was that social change is _____ and progressive.

14. _____ theorists ask how social structure serves the interests of various compelling groups within a society.

15. An ethnic group is a good example of a _____ group.

16. In cultures that possess a _____ rule of residence, newlyweds reside near or with the bride's family.

17. Paige's research demonstrated a very strong correlation between rules of residence and _____.

18.* A(n) _____ gathers information from every person in the population.

19. When correlations are _____ the regression line slopes from lower left to upper right.

20.* Sampling that proceeds through a series of levels is termed _____ sampling.

*Note: These questions are drawn from Special Topic 1.

Multiple Choice

1. Research by Darley and Latenè found:
   a. the larger the group present, the more an individual will feel personal responsibility to act in an emergency
   b. the larger the group present, the less an individual will feel personal responsibility to act in an emergency
   c. the size of the group present has no effect on bystander apathy
   d. church attendence and delinquency rates are inversely correlated
   e. none of the above

2. Survey research:
   a. collects data using questionnaires and personal interviews
   b. uses samples
   c. can establish time order more easily than experiments can
   d. a and b
   e. all of the above

3. When sex differences were controlled, Hirschi and Stark found that:
   a. boys who attend church are less likely to be delinquents than are boys who did not attend church
   b. girls who attend church are less likely to be delinquents than are girls who did not attend church
   c. the more people present at an emergency, the more likely the victim is to receive help
   d. a and b
   e. none of the above

4. Research on delinquency and religion has found that:
   a. religion is negatively correlated with delinquency in schools where the majority of the students are religious
   b. religion is positively correlated with delinquency in schools where the majority of the students are religious
   c. religion is negatively correlated with delinquency in schools where most students are not religious
   d. religion is positively correlated with delinquency in schools where most students are not religious
   e. there was no correlation between religion and delinquency in schools where most of the students are religious

5. Elements of systems include:
   a. separate parts or structures
   b. interdependence among parts
   c. equilibrium among the parts
   d. b and c
   e. all of the above

6. Basic institutions found in all societies include:
   a. the family
   b. the political order
   c. religion
   d. a and c
   e. all of the above

7. Macro sociologists assume:
   a. societies are never wholly static
   b. every structure is related to every other structure
   c. the same degree of interdependence among structures exists in all societies
   d. b and c
   e. all of the above

8. _____ theories explain social structures on the basis of their consequences for other parts of the system.
   a. conflict
   b. functional
   c. social evolution
   d. symbolic interaction
   e. choice

9. Arrangements among structures that harm or distort the system are termed _____.
   a. functional alternatives
   b. functional requisites
   c. dysfunctions
   d. latent functions
   e. manifest functions

10. Contemporary evolutionary theories:
    a. always assume that all societies evolve to more complex cultures
    b. are meant to apply to the population of cases
    c. assume that all change is inevitable and progressive
    d. all of the above
    e. none of the above

11. _____ theorists ask how social structure serves the interests of various competing groups within a society.
    a. functional
    b. conflict
    c. social evolutionary
    d. micro
    e. choice

12. The term *status group* is most closely associated with:
   a. Marx
   b. Weber
   c. Lenski
   d. Paige
   e. Darley

13. Macro sociological research must always be based on:
   a. individuals
   b. the comparative study of groups
   c. case studies
   d. primitive societies
   e. none of the above

14. Societies with factional politics:
   a. reach decisions through competition and conflict
   b. stress agreement rather than disagreement
   c. contain internal groups that stress their own interests
   d. a and c
   e. none of the above

15. When Paige examined primitive societies, he found that:
   a. kinship and residence are primary bases for group formation
   b. conflict occurs primarily among men of different kinship groups
   c. patrilocal societies were often more communal than matrilocal societies
   d. a and b
   e. all of the above

16. Societies in which the bride leaves home after marriage and the couple takes up residence with or close to the husband's family have a _____ rule of residence.
   a. matrilocal
   b. neolocal
   c. patrilocal
   d. fratralocal
   e. nuclear

17. Paige's study of structure and conflict used _____.
   a. field research
   b. the experimental method
   c. comparative research
   d. simple random samples
   e. none of the above

18.* Which of the following is/are true?
   a. correlations can be positive or negative
   b. when there is no correlation the regression line slopes from upper left to lower right
   c. the closer the correlation coefficient is to 1.00 the less the correlation between the two measures
   d. a and c
   e. all of the above

19.* The odds that a sample will be like the whole population depend on:
   a. the absolute size of the sample
   b. the ratio of the sample size to the population size
   c. the use of stratified rather than simple random samples
   d. a and b
   e. all of the above

20. Which of the following is *not* correctly paired with his or her contribution?
   a. Darley and Latenè—bystander apathy
   b. Karl Marx—social evolutionary theory
   c. Max Weber—status group
   d. Paige—comparative study of family systems of primitive societies
   e. b and c above

*Note: Questions 18 and 19 are drawn from the Special Topic on sampling.

Essay

1. A. Explain functional and conflict theories. (comprehension)
   B. Attempt to integrate functional and conflict theories into a more general explanation of society. (application)
   C. *Compare and contrast* functional and conflict theories. (analysis)

2. A. Define micro and macro sociology. (knowledge)
   B. Explain the relationship between micro and macro sociology. (comprehension)
   C. Show how the research on religion and delinquency illustrates this relationship. (application)

3. Briefly discuss the research findings of Stark and others on religion and delinquency.

4. Using examples, discuss the three elements of a system.

5. Discuss Paige's research on kinship structure and political conflict.

Answers

Completion
1. less
2. survey research
3. spurious
4. social structures
5. macro
6. equilibrium
7. education, family, the economy
8. institutions, needs
9. nuclear
10. functional alternative
11. dysfunctions
12. social evolutionary
13. inevitable
14. conflict
15. status
16. matrilocal
17. political conflict
18. census
19. positive
20. stratified random

Multiple Choice
1. b
2. d
3. e
4. e
5. e
6. e
7. a
8. b
9. c
10. b
11. b
12. b
13. b
14. d
15. d
16. c
17. c
18. a
19. a
20. b

Review and Special Project

Review

Chapters 1 through 4 have introduced sociology, discussing it as a science and introducing many new concepts central to sociology. They have discussed both micro and macro sociology and the theory and research in these areas.

You may wish to test your knowledge of this material by actually trying your hand at doing some sociology. Although it might be difficult to conduct a study in a few weeks without administrative and financial backing, it is possible to design one. Through this design you will test your knowledge of several areas and obtain first-hand knowledge of sociology in action.

Special Project

Using students on your campus as subjects, assume you want to replicate one of the following studies: Ofshe's study of attachments and conformity, Milgram's "small world" research, or one of the studies on religion and delinquency conducted by Stark and others. Design a study based on the original study you have chosen.

As you design your study, be certain to address the following questions:

1. What did the original researcher hypothesize and what were the results?
2. What do you hypothesize? Do you expect similar results?
3. Is your research experimental or nonexperimental?
4. How will you draw your sample? What kind will you use?
5. What method will you use to gather your data?
6. How will you establish the criteria of causation?
7. Is your study more in the realm of micro or macro sociology?
8. Does your study use the assumptions of any particular theory? What are they?
9. Can you identify any problems or issues that might arise if you actually were to conduct this study? How might you address them in advance?

CHAPTER FIVE

Biology, Culture, and Society

Overview

Chapter 5 starts with a brief historical discussion of instinctual and environmental theories of behavior. It explains behavioral genetics and shows how most social scientists today take a balanced position between heredity and environment. Research such as the numerous twin studies is cited to support the notion of interplay between biology and environment. After intelligence testing is discussed, the issue of race and intelligence is raised, with a brief summary of Jensen's controversy. The chapter then focuses on a discussion of research findings from ethology on learned behavior among animals. Jane Goodall's pioneering research with chimpanzees is cited as the "over-the-shoulder" example. The chapter closes with a discussion of symbolic communication in primates.

Capsule Summary

Early in this century **instinctual theories** dominated the social sciences. They postulated that behavior was **inborn** and the result of **heredity**. By the 1930s, however, **environmental theories** dominated. They postulated that behavior was strictly the result of **cultural** and **social** influences, with **biology** playing no role.

Today most social scientists assume that humans are the result of the interplay between their **biology** and their **social** and **cultural** environments. (The concepts **genotype** and **phenotype** illustrate this interplay.) Indeed, the rapidly growing field of **behavioral genetics** seeks to identify **traits** that **influence behavior** and have some **genetic basis**. Research in this area has emphasized the study of **identical twins**, particularly identical twins **reared apart**. These twins often exhibit **similar, although not identical, characteristics**. Similarly, the interplay of heredity and environment is illustrated by the research of **Tanner** and others on the **increasing physical size** and the **decline** in the **age of the onset of puberty** of Europeans and Americans over the past century. They found that **environmental conditions** can suppress **genetic potential**.

Intelligence testing began with **Binet**, who developed what was to become the **Stanford-Binet Test of Intelligence**. This test and others compare a person's **mental age** with his or her **calendar age** to determine an **intelligence quotient**. IQ tests have proved to be powerful predictors of academic or career success and tend to vary little over a person's life. **IQ** testing came under criticism, particularly when **Jensen** published a highly controversial article, which argued that the differences between the **scores** of **blacks** and **whites** were the result of **genetic** differences. **Sowell**, in an ingenious study, determined that the differences were due instead to **environmental** and **cultural suppression of innate potential**, thus illustrating again the interplay between heredity and environment.

Sociologists have long assumed that humans differ from other animals in that we **alone possess culture and language**. Recent studies in **ethology** by field researchers such as **Jane Goodall** have discovered evidence of **learned behavior, tool making**, and use of **symbolic communication** among other animals, particularly primates. The **Harlows'** research with **monkeys** showed that **early isolation** had **detrimental effects** on adult **behavior** such as **sexual performance** and **social relationships**. A landmark in the **study of communication** was reached when the **Gardiners** taught a chimp, **Washoe**, American sign language. **Washoe** was able to **communicate** through **sign language** and eventually to **teach these signs** to another infant chimp placed in her care.

Key Concepts

You should be prepared to explain the concepts and terms listed here, as well as give several examples of each concept.

Instinct 120	Phenotype 123
Chromosome 123	Intelligence quotient (IQ) 131
Gene 123	Language 136
Genotype 123	Tool 139

Key Research Studies

You should be familiar with both the methodology and the results of these research studies.

Rosenthal, Schuckit, and others: twin studies 126
Tanner: declining age of the onset of puberty 127
Jensen: controversial study of race and IQ 134
Sowell: response to Jensen, race, IQ, and immigrant status 134
Goodall: field research with chimpanzees 137
Harlow and Harlow: effects of isolation on infant monkeys 140
Gardiner and Gardiner: teaching American sign language to chimps 142

Key Figures

Be able to associate each of the following with his or her contribution and explain any concepts or theories associated with him or her.

William McDougall: social psychologist who proposed instinctual theory
Alfred Binet: Stanford-Binet Test of Intelligence
Jane Goodall: study of wild chimps
Washoe: first chimp to learn American sign language

Key Theories

You should be able to explain the assumptions of these theories and, when applicable, cite related research findings.

Instinctual theory
Environmental theory
Behavioral genetics

Completion

1. A(n) _____ is a form of behavior that occurs in all normal members of a species without having been learned.

2. The major proponent of instinctual theories was the social psychologist_____.

3. By the 1930s the social sciences were dominated by purely _____ theories.

4. Today we take the position that human beings are the result of the interplay between their _____ and their _____.

5. In our chromosomes are tiny structures termed _____, which contain DNA.

6. The phenotype is the actual outcome of the interplay between the _____ and the environment.

7. Tanner found that the age of the onset of menstruation has _____ in Europe and the United States over the past century.

8. Intelligence testing was begun by the French psychologist _____.

9. An intelligence quotient is a person's _____ age divided by the calendar age multiplied by 100.

10. It has been found that IQ tests are powerful predictors of _____ and _____.

11. In 1969 Jensen argued that interracial differences in average IQ were the result of _____.

12. A _____ is an object that has been modified to suit a particular purpose.

13. Older introductory texts have often argued that humans differ from other animals in that only humans possess _____ and _____.

14. Students of animal behavior are termed _____.

47

15. _____ argued that lower IQ scores among blacks are the result of environmental suppression of innate potential.

16. The Harlows' study of monkeys found that many of the effects of early isolation seem _____.

17. Goodall discovered both toolmaking and _____ among the chimps in the wild.

18. The Gardiners taught Washoe to communicate through the use of _____.

19. It is widely recognized that much nonhuman behavior is _____ although much is also learned.

20. A virtue of animal studies is that we can manipulate _____ to study adaptation.

Multiple Choice

1. Early instinctual theories:
   a. discounted the impact of cultural and social influences on human development
   b. dominated social science during the 1930s
   c. assigned no role to heredity
   d. b and c
   e. all of the above

2. The major proponent of instinctual theories was:
   a. Thomas Sowell
   b. Alfred Binet
   c. William McDougall
   d. James Tanner
   e. Arthur Jensen

3. Today most social scientists take the premise that human development results from:
   a. purely environmental influences
   b. purely biological influences
   c. an interplay between biology and environment
   d. purely cultural influences
   e. none of the above

4. The sum total of the genetic instructions that an organism receives from its parents is called the:
   a. genotype
   b. chromosomal number
   c. phenotype
   d. geno-number
   e. pheno-number

5. Behavioral geneticists have claimed considerable success in isolating human characteristics and behavior that are influenced to a substantial degree by genetic inheritance. Some of these include:
    a. alcoholism
    b. intelligence
    c. a tendency toward impulsive and aggressive behavior
    d. a and c
    e. all of the above

6. Studies of identical twins reared apart have found their IQs to be:
    a. identical
    b. extremely similar
    c. markedly different
    d. unmeasurable
    e. none of the above; no such subjects have been discovered

7. Social consequences of early maturation include:
    a. an increase in the age at marriage compared with the past century
    b. more permissive attitudes toward premarital sex
    c. a need for adult authority to be based on something other than size
    d. b and c
    e. all of the above

8. The recent increased acceptance of premarital sexual activity has resulted from:
    a. earlier sexual maturity
    b. more reliable methods of contraception
    c. legalized abortion
    d. b and c
    e. all of the above

9. Research has found that people in America and Europe are _____ than they did in the past century:
    a. achieving puberty earlier
    b. growing and reaching their full size later
    c. marrying much later
    d. a and c
    e. all of the above

10. Intelligence testing was developed by:
    a. Arthur Jensen
    b. Alfred Binet
    c. Thomas Sowell
    d. John Stanford
    e. b and d

11. If a person's mental age is 25 percent higher than his/her calendar age, that person's IQ is:
   a.   100
   b.   125
   c.   75
   d.   115
   e.   150

12. IQ tests:
   a.   have been found to be good indicators of school performance
   b.   are very consistent over the person's life
   c.   were seldom administered before 1950
   d.   a and b
   e.   all of the above

13. Jensen argued that the differences between the IQ scores of blacks and whites was the result of:
   a.   environmental differences
   b.   genetic differences
   c.   environmental suppression of the genotype
   d.   invalid testing instruments
   e.   cultural deprivation

14. Sowell's research found that the differences in the IQ scores of blacks and whites were due to:
   a.   genetic differences
   b.   innate racial characteristics
   c.   environmental suppression of innate potential
   d.   a and b
   e.   an invalid testing instrument

15. Sowell argued that IQ tests:
   a.   were invalid when used on black children
   b.   can reflect how social and cultural deprivation can damage people's abilities
   c.   should be discontinued
   d.   a and c
   e.   none of the above

16. Ethologists study:
   a.   primitive societies
   b.   the interplay between environment and biology in humans
   c.   animal behavior
   d.   genetic potential in humans
   e.   none of the above

17. The Harlows found that monkeys reared in total isolation:
    a. were no different from monkeys reared with other monkeys
    b. made up for early deficits when they joined monkey colonies
    c. were unable to engage in social and sexual relationships
    d. a and b
    e. none of the above

18. Jane Goodall discovered that chimpanzees in the wild:
    a. make and use tools
    b. communicate through sign language
    c. kill and eat other animals
    d. a and c
    e. all of the above

19. Advantages of primate studies include:
    a. we can manipulate the environment to study adaptation
    b. we can observe primates as substitutes for our most ancient ancestors
    c. we can seek basic elements of social organization by examining societies that have
       not been overlaid with a great deal of culture
    d. all of the above
    e. none of the above

20. The case of Washoe illustrates that:
    a. chimp behavior is determined entirely by instincts
    b. chimps can learn sign language but cannot use it to form sentences
    c. chimps cannot transmit language to their young
    d. chimps can learn to speak words
    e. none of the above

Essay

1. A. Distinguish between genotypes and phenotypes. (knowledge)
    B. Explain the following statement: "Human beings are a result of the interplay
       between their biology and their social and cultural environment." (comprehension)
    C. Give an example of a human behavior or characteristic, and show how it is the
       result of the interrelationship between genetic inheritance and the environment.
       (application)

2. A. Explain instinctual and environmental theories. (comprehension)
    B. Using current research, interrelate the role of heredity and environment.
       (application)
    C. Contrast instinctual and environmental theories. (analysis)

3. Discuss the race and IQ controversy. Show how Jensen's argument was countered by Sowell's research findings.

4. Show how Tanner's research illustrates the interplay between biology and environment.

5. Using the research studies on primates, show how these research findings do not support the premise that humans alone possess culture and can communicate through a formal system.

Answers

Completion
1. Instinct
2. William McDougall
3. environmental
4. biology, social and cultural environment
5. genes
6. genotype
7. declined
8. Alfred Binet
9. mental
10. school performance, occupational success
11. genetic differences
12. tool
13. culture and language
14. ethologists
15. Thomas Sowell
16. irreversible
17. meat eating (killing)
18. American sign language
19. instinctive
20. environment

Multiple Choice
1. a
2. c
3. c
4. a
5. e
6. b
7. d
8. e
9. a
10. b
11. b
12. d
13. b
14. c
15. b
16. c
17. c
18. e
19. d
20. c

CHAPTER SIX

Socialization and Social Roles

Overview

This chapter introduces the process of socialization and describes research findings on the effects of early isolation and deprivation as evidence of the importance of this process. Piaget's work on cognitive development is discussed in depth. Brown and Bellugi's work on language acquisition is also included in the discussion of cognitive structures. The relationship between interaction and cognitive development with an emphasis on the "attachment teaching hypothesis" is discussed. Emotional development, the emergence of the self, and personality development are described. Chapter 6 then turns its attention to the theory of cultural determinism, its assumptions, research findings, and recent criticisms. Margaret Mead's famous works provide examples of extreme cultural determinism. Differential socialization is discussed, and Kohn's research in this area is highlighted as the "over-the-shoulder" example. Goffman's "stage analogy" of interaction is described with examples of his concepts. The chapter closes with a discussion of the origins and current status of differential socialization on the basis of gender.

Capsule Summary

Socialization is the crucial learning process that allows us to possess **culture** and participate in **social relations**. **Feral children** are examples of extreme isolation and deprivation. Early studies such as those by **Skeels and Dye** documented the importance of interaction and contact during the early years.

For many years psychology was dominated by the **stimulus-response** (SR) theory of learning. It argued that **behavior** was a response to **external stimuli** and that **learning** was a result of **reinforcement**. Piaget took issue with the SR theory and argued that the human mind develops and functions on the basis of **cognitive structures**. Through extensive research he proposed the existence of **four stages** of **cognitive development**: **sensorimotor**, **preoperational**, **concrete operational**, and **formal operational**. Children in these stages differ in their ability to comprehend concepts and situations. Others who endorsed the concept of cognitive structures include **Brown and Bellugi**, whose research on **language acquisition** indicated that young children's speech often seems to indicate a search for grammatical rules.

Piaget has been criticized for ignoring the role of **social interaction** in his work. Recent research has focused on the relationship between **verbal interaction** and **language acquisition** (the "attachment—teaching hypothesis"), and this research has yielded some surprising results.

An important aspect of the **socialization process** is the emergence of the self. Research by **Bain**, **Flavell**, and **others** has expanded on earlier work by **Piaget** and **Mead**. **Personality** refers to the consistent pattern of **thoughts, feelings,** and **actions** displayed by an individual. **Personality** emphasizes both the **similarities** and the **differences** among individuals.

    Cultural determinism was a dominant theory in anthropology in the 1920s and 1930s. In its extreme form, cultural determinism argues that **personality** is totally shaped by **culture** and that **child-rearing practices** are critical in determining later **personality** characteristics. **Mead's** works on **adolescence** in **Samoa** and on **sex and temperament** are classic examples of **cultural determinism.** These studies have recently come under criticism, and today most social scientists take the position that culture and early socialization are important in shaping personality but are not the only factors.

    Because not all people in a society are expected to play identical roles, not all members of a society are socialized exactly the same. **Differential socialization** accounts for some of the differences among people. **Kohn's** study, for example, found that **parents often socialize** their children on the **basis of the roles** that they **expect them to perform.** These expectations often reflect the **parents' own working conditions.**

    Erving Goffman studied interaction from the point of view that the world is a stage on which we are all actors. He distinguished between **role** and **role performance** and used concepts such as **props, front stage** and **backstage,** and **impression management** in his analogy.

    Differential socialization is possibly best illustrated in **sex-role socialization.** Although the sexes do **differ biologically,** these differences were a more important basis for the **assignment** of **roles** in **primitive societies** than they are at **present.** These early societies laid the foundation for differential socialization by gender that has become a part of our culture. Today we still **socialize males** and **females differently.**

    Research by **DeLoache et al.** found that when reading to their children, **mothers assign gender** to **neutral characters** in children's books. These assignments are typically based on conventional **sex role stereotypes.** Likewise, **Richer** found that **gender** plays a significant role in older children's choice of playmates.

Key Concepts

You should be able to explain the following concepts. You should also be able to cite several examples of each concept.

Key Research Studies

You should be familiar with both the methodology and the results of these research studies.

Skeels and Dye: early study of the effects of socialization on retardation   148

Brown and Bellugi and others: language acquisition of children   153

Bretherton et al.: "attachment—teaching hypothesis"   154

Bain and others: the emergence of the self   155

Margaret Mead: anthropological studies supporting cultural determinism—*Coming of Age in Samoa, Sex and Temperament*   158

Melvin Kohn: relationship among social class, parental expectation of role, and socialization   161

Juhasz: self-esteem among junior high students   166

DeLoache et al: assignment of gender to neutral characters in children's books   167

Richer: games and gender   168

Key Figures

Be able to associate each person with his or her contribution.

Erving Goffman: role performance, front and back stage behavior, studied nonobservance, and impression management

Jean Piaget: theory of cognitive stages

Franz Boaz: anthropologist; theory of cultural determinism

Margaret Mead: anthropologist; theory of cultural determinism

Key Theories

You should be able to explain the assumptions of these theories and, when applicable, to cite related research findings.

Stimulus-response

Theory of cognitive stages

Cultural determinism

Completion

1. Children who are neglected and isolated from human contact are termed _____.

2. The learning process by which infants become normal human beings, possessed of culture and able to participate in social relations, is termed _____.

3. Socialization related to roles and to _____ is termed differential socialization.

4. The theory that behavior is merely a response to external stimuli and that we repeat whatever behavior has been reinforced by our environment is termed _____.

5. Piaget argued that the human mind develops and functions on the basis of _____ or general rules for reasoning.

6. Piaget's cognitive stages include the _____, preoperational, concrete operational, and _____.

7. The rule of _____ is Piaget's term for the principle that objects continue to exist even when they are out of sight.

8. The third stage in Piaget's theory of cognitive development is _____.

9. Researchers have concluded that perhaps _____ of all adults do not reach the formal operations stage.

10. Brown and Bellugi found that young children experiment with speech in ways that appear to involve a search for _____.

11. An individual's consistent pattern of thoughts, feelings, and actions are termed his/her _____.

12. _____ published and taught the theory of cultural determinism.

13. Mead described the _____ as gentle, unaggressive, and passive and argued that both men and women have "feminine temperaments."

14. _____ published both *Coming of Age in Samoa* and *Sex and Temperament in Three Primitive Societies*.

15. Kohn found that in contrast to working-class parents, middle-class parents were more concerned about their children being capable of _____ and _____.

16. A study in which observations are made of the same people at several different times is termed a _____ study.

17. The actual conduct of a particular individual while on duty in a position is termed _____.

18. Goffman termed "the conscious manipulation of role performance" _____.

19. A set of norms attached to a position that, in turn, violates the norms adhered to by the larger society is termed a _____.

20. DeLoach et al. found that mothers were most likely to attribute _____ identities to gender-neutral characters.

Multiple Choice

1. The socialization process:
   a. is a learning process
   b. begins at birth and ends at age 7
   c. literally means to be "made social"
   d. a and c
   e. all of the above

2. Skeels and Dye found that infants who had been placed under the personal care of an older girl showed _____ when compared with those who remained in the orphanage.
   a. slight improvement
   b. dramatic improvement
   c. no improvement
   d. slight decline in ability
   e. marked decline in ability

3. The stimulus-response theory postulated that learning results from:
   a. reinforcement
   b. cognitive structures
   c. developmental stages
   d. instincts
   e. heredity

4. The first stage of cognitive development is the:
   a. preoperational
   b. formal operational
   c. sensorimotor
   d. concrete operational
   e. sensorioperational

5. During the preoperational stage, children lack:
   a. the rule of object permanence
   b. the rule of conservation
   c. the ability to put themselves in someone else's place
   d. b and c
   e. all of the above

6. Researchers estimate that about _____ of all adults do not reach the formal operations stage.
   a. one-fourth
   b. one-third
   c. one-half
   d. two-thirds
   e. three-quarters

7. In their study of language acquisition, Brown and Bellugi discovered that:
   a. young children's speech contains only the most vital words
   b. parents frequently echo their children, thus expanding and correcting their sentences
   c. young children experiment with speech in ways that seem to involve a search for grammatical rules
   d. a and c
   e. all of the above

8. Research in the area of the "attachment-teaching hypothesis" has shown:
   a. kids who are exposed to motherese acquire language much more rapidly than those who are not
   b. kids who are talked to learn to talk sooner and better
   c. the degree of attachments a child enjoys plays a major role in language acquisition
   d. all of the above
   e. none of the above

9. In terms of their personalities:
   a. all humans are alike in some ways
   b. all humans are like only some other humans
   c. all humans are unique in some ways
   d. b and c
   e. all of the above

10. The principle of cultural determinism argues that:
    a. individuals' personalities are tiny replicas of their cultures
    b. are the result of an interplay between biology and culture
    c. are totally the result of heredity
    d. are not well developed among primitive people
    e. none of the above

11. The theory of cultural determinism is most closely associated with:
    a. Jean Piaget
    b. Franz Boaz
    c. Roger Brown
    d. Melvin Kohn
    e. Erving Goffman

12. Margaret Mead argued that the differences in temperament between the Arapesh and the Mundugumor were the result of:
    a. innate biological differences
    b. child-rearing practices, especially during infancy
    c. the physical location of their respective societies
    d. b and c
    e. none of the above

13. In his *initial* study, Kohn found that middle-class parents typically stressed the value(s) of:
   a. self-expression
   b. independence
   c. conformity
   d. a and b
   e. all of the above

14. In his *later* studies, Kohn found that parents differed in their child-rearing practices *primarily* on the basis of the parents':
   a. social class
   b. work conditions
   c. educational level
   d. a and c
   e. none of the above

15. In a longitudinal study observations are made of:
   a. different people at several different times
   b. different people at the same time
   c. the same people at several different times
   d. nonhuman animals in natural settings
   e. none of the above

16. Goffman termed "the conscious manipulation of scenery, props, costumes, and our behavior in order to convey a particular role image to others":
   a. role failure
   b. studied nonobservance
   c. impression management
   d. backstage behavior
   e. teamwork

17. When we pretend not to see miscues in others' role performance we are practicing:
   a. role failure
   b. studied nonobservance
   c. impression management
   d. backstage behavior
   e. teamwork

18. Juhasz's study of self-esteem of 7th and 8th graders found that _____ has a potent effect on self-conceptions.
   a. gender
   b. academic abilities
   c. parental occupation
   d. religion
   e. none of the above

19. Research by DeLoache et al. found that the subjects in the study:
    a. typically referred to the gender-neutral characters as males
    b. typically referred to the gender-neutral characters as females
    c. always identified the "teachers" as female and the "drivers" as male
    d. a and c
    e. none of the above

20. Richer's results suggest:
    a. older children display gender preferences in their play, but younger children don't
    b. older children do not display gender differences in their play
    c. the gender preferences of the slightly older children seem to be innate
    d. a and c
    e. none of the above

Essay

1. A. List Piaget's four stages of cognitive development. (knowledge)
   B. Describe these stages using examples. (comprehension)
   C. Contrast the type of thinking characteristic of a child in the preoperational stage with that of a child in the concrete operations stages. (analysis)

2. A. Explain the stimulus-response theory of learning. (knowledge)
   B. Show how the work of Piaget or of Brown and Bellugi does not support the assumptions of SR theory.
   C. Design a study to test Piaget's theory, or replicate the work of Brown and Bellugi. (application)

3. Explain cultural determinism. Discuss Mead's studies as an example of extreme cultural determinism.

4. Discuss some of the recent criticisms of Mead's work. Explain the contemporary position held by most sociologists regarding the relationship between culture and personality.

5. Explain differential socialization. Discuss Kohn's work in this area.

Answers

Completion
1. feral children
2. socialization
3. role expectations
4. stimulus-response
5. cognitive structures
6. sensorimotor, formal operational
7. object permanence
8. concrete operational stage management
9. one-half (50 percent)
10. grammatical rules
11. personality
12. Boaz
13. Arapesh
14. Margaret Mead
15. self-expression, independence
16. longitudinal
17. role performance
18. impression
19. deviant role
20. male (or masculine)

Multiple Choice
1. d
2. b
3. a
4. c
5. d
6. c
7. e
8. b
9. e
10. a
11. b
12. b
13. d
14. b
15. c
16. c
17. b
18. a
19. a
20. a

CHAPTER SEVEN

Deviance and Conformity

Overview

Chapter 7 begins with an introduction to deviant behavior, discussing both early and contemporary biological theories of deviance and related research findings. Personality theory and its relationship to aggressive behavior is then discussed as an example of a psychological approach. Sociological theories are introduced with a brief discussion of importance of attachments. The chapter then discusses in depth the major sociological theories of deviance: differential association/social learning, subcultural deviation, structural strain, control theory, anomie, and labeling. In each case, the major assumptions of the theory are considered, relevant research findings are cited, and shortcomings and criticisms of the theory are noted. In the discussion of control theory, Crutchfield and Stark's study of crime rates and moral and social integration is described as the "over-the-shoulder" example. The chapter ends with an attempt to combine key elements of all the major sociological theories into a more general theory of deviance.

Capsule Summary

Behavior that violates norms is termed **deviant behavior**. Serious deviance depends on both the **importance** of the norm that was violated and the **frequency** of norm violation. Distinctions can be made between **intentional** deviance, which involves **rational calculation**, and **duration** and **impulsive** deviance, which **lacks** these **criteria**.

There are sociological and nonsociological theories of deviation. **Biological** theories attempt to show how deviants differ physically from nondeviants. **Lombroso's** theory of "born criminals" and the more recent approach of **Gove** (age, gender, biology, and deviance) are examples of biological explanations. Similarly, most **psychological research** has been unable to find a significant relationship between **personality** type and **deviance**, although recent studies do indicate a possible link between **violent behavior** and **self-esteem**.

Sociological theories of deviance include **differential association/social learning, subcultural deviance, structural strain, control theory, anomie, and labeling**. Each of these is based on different assumptions, and each has certain shortcomings.

Sutherland's theory of **differential association** argues that deviant behavior, like other behavior, is learned through socialization. Thus, attachments to others who are deviant may encourage deviation. Later learning theories have included the concept of **selective reinforcement** to explain this process further.

Subcultural deviance emphasizes the **conflicts over norms**, which may arise in a society that contains many subcultures. Thus, behavior that may be conforming in a deviant subculture may be deviant to the general culture.

Merton's theory of **structural strain** argues that **deviance results** from the **frustrations** experienced by those who occupy **disadvantaged positions** in the **stratification system**. It argues that in attempting to **conform** to culturally **approved goals** the poor will find the legitimate means to these **goals blocked** and hence will resort to **illegitimate deviant means** to attain them. A major shortcoming of strain theory is that it is unable to explain high rates of **white collar crime** present in society.

Attempting to explain **conformity** rather than **deviance, control theory** argues that conformity is tied to the bonds between an individual and the group. If the bonds are strong, the individual is more likely to conform. It recognizes the existence of four types of bonds— **attachments, involvements, investments,** and **belief**—and argues that an individual is likely to deviate when these bonds are weak.

Anomie (literally "normlessness") argues that deviance is the result of **low social** and **moral integration**. This idea was first proposed by Durkheim in his discussion of "moral communities." Recent studies by **Crutchfield** and **Stark** have found significant relationships between the **degree** of **social** and **moral integration** of an area and **crimes** that involve **intentional deviance**.

Labeling theory distinguishes between **primary** and **secondary** deviation and focuses on the **effect** that a **deviant label** has on both the **recipient** and the society. It argues that **labels are not uniformly applied** to all deviants and that ultimately the **label itself** may cause a **return to deviant behavior**.

Each of these theories contains elements useful in explaining deviance. Similarly, each has shortcomings and criticisms. To construct a general theory of deviation, therefore, elements of all these theories should be integrated into a more complete explanation.

Key Concepts

You should be able to explain the concepts listed here. Be prepared to cite several examples of each concept.

Key Research Studies

Be familiar with both the methodology and the results of the following research studies.
    Gove: age, gender, biology, and deviance   177
    Berkowitz: relationship between aggressive behavior and self-esteem   180
    Linden and Fillmore: delinquency study in Canada (combination of differential association and control theory)   191
    Crutchfield: social integration and crime rates   194
    Stark: moral integration and crime rates   195

Key Figures

You should be able to associate each person with his contribution.
    Cesare Lombroso: father of modern criminology; "born criminals"
    Edwin Sutherland: theory of differential association
    Robert Burgess and Ronald Akers: social learning (refined differential association)
    Robert K. Merton: strain theory; relationship between cultural means and goals
    Emile Durkheim: control theory; anomie

Key Theories

Know how to explain the assumptions of these theories and, when applicable, cite related research findings.
    Biological theory of deviance
    Personality (psychological) theory of deviance
    Differential association (social learning)
    Subcultural deviance
    Structural strain
    Control theory
    Anomie
    Labeling

Completion

1. Behavior that does not conform to norms is termed _____.

2. Serious deviance depends not only on the _____ of the norm violated but also on the _____ of norm violation.

3. The concept of "born criminal" is associated with _____.

4. Gove argued that physically demanding forms of deviant behavior are overwhelmingly committed by _____.

5. Berkowitz found a relationship between aggressive behavior and _____.

6. Sutherland proposed the theory of _____, which argued that all behavior is the result of socialization by means of interaction.

7. Subculture deviance can be explained as conflicts over _____.

8. _____ theories attempt to explain deviance on the basis of frustration caused by a person's position in the social structure.

9. _____ argued that deviance is a built-in consequence of stratification.

10. The initial assumption made by all _____ theories is that life is a vast cafeteria of temptation.

11. For control theory, the causes of conformity are the _____ between an individual and the group.

12. Types of social bonds include _____, _____, beliefs, and involvements.

13. Anomie is a condition of _____.

14. Durkheim argued that moral communities are characterized by moral integration and _____.

15. Crutchfield's study focused on the relationship between crime rates and _____.

16. _____ deviance involves rational calculation and duration.

17. Secondary deviance is a reaction to having been _____.

18. _____ deviance lacks calculation and duration.

19. Stark, et al. argue that sociological theories of deviance should apply only to instances of _____ deviance.

20. _____ deviation involves actions that cause others to label an individual as deviant.

Multiple Choice

1. Serious deviance depends on:
   a. the importance of the norm violated
   b. the age of the violator
   c. the frequency of norm violation
   d. a and c
   e. all of the above

2. Which of the following statements is/are true?
   a. some actions are regarded as deviant only in some societies
   b. in all societies some people commit acts of serious deviance
   c. all societies punish their deviants
   d. a and b
   e. all of the above

3. According to Lombroso's theory, violent criminals:
   a. differ biologically from noncriminals
   b. have low self-esteem
   c. are under age 30
   d. experience frustration caused by poverty
   e. learn crime in association with other criminals

4. Sutherland's theory of differential association attributed deviance to:
   a. biological differences between deviants and nondeviants
   b. low self-esteem
   c. strain or frustration caused by poverty
   d. being labeled deviant
   e. attachments to others who are deviant

5. Gove's research revealed:
   a. the arrest rate for violent crimes is highest for ages 25–30
   b. females are more likely to be arrested for violent crimes than males
   c. the arrest rate for violent crimes drops markedly after age 30
   d. a and c
   e. all of the above

6. Berkowitz found that men who commit violent acts such as assault:
   a. are biologically different from those who do not
   b. have low self-esteem
   c. were often members of deviant subcultures
   d. were very passive people who had suppressed their aggression too long
   e. none of the above

7. Differential association theory is most closely associated with:
   a. Cesare Lombroso
   b. Robert Merton
   c. Edwin Sutherland
   d. Emile Durkheim
   e. Leonard Berkowitz

8. Subcultural deviance:
   a. can be explained as conflicts over norms
   b. lets us understand that deviance is often a matter of definition
   c. explains deviation both among and within subcultural groups
   d. a and b
   e. all of the above

9. Which of the following men is/are not correctly matched with his theory?
   a. Sutherland: differential association
   b. Merton: subcultural deviance
   c. Durkheim: anomie
   d. Lombroso: born criminals
   e. b and c

10. Structural strain theory attempts to explain deviance as a response to:
    a. a deviant label that stigmatizes a person
    b. conflicts over norms
    c. a low rate of moral integration
    d. deviant attachments
    e. none of the above

11. Problems with strain theory include:
    a. studies have found that a person's social class is barely, if at all, related to committing crimes
    b. the theory seems to predict less deviance than actually occurs
    c. the theory offers no explanation for deviant behavior committed by those in poverty
    d. a and c
    e. all of the above

12. Bonds between the individual and the group include:
    a. attachments
    b. beliefs
    c. investments
    d. a and c
    e. all of the above

13. Control theory argues that deviant behavior is more likely to occur when:
    a. people have less to gain from deviance than from conformity
    b. an individual spends a good deal of time and effort on activities that conform to the norms
    c. the bonds between the individual and the group are weak
    d. a and b
    e. none of the above

14. The costs we have expended in constructing a satisfactory life and the current and potential flow of rewards coming to us are termed:
    a. investments
    b. involvements
    c. attachments
    d. beliefs
    e. none of the above

15. Linden and Fillmore's study of delinquency found:
    a. attachments to parents and liking school were negatively correlated with being delinquent
    b. attachments to parents and liking school were positively correlated with having delinquent friends
    c. attachments to delinquent peers greatly increase the level of delinquency
    d. a and c
    e. b and c

16. According to Durkheim, moral communities are characterized by:
    a. high rates of moral integration
    b. high rates of anomie
    c. shared beliefs, especially religious beliefs
    d. a and c
    e. none of the above

17. Research by Crutchfield and Stark has found that moral and social integration:
    a. can inhibit impulsive deviance
    b. can limit intentional deviance
    c. can limit all types of crime
    d. do not affect crime rates
    e. none of the above

18. Mizruchi has suggested the term _____ as the best translation of anomie into English.
    a. social disorganization
    b. deregulation
    c. moral disorganization
    d. role failure
    e. none of the above

19. Impulsive deviance:
    a. lacks calculation and duration
    b. involves rational calculation and duration
    c. can easily be explained by sociological theories
    d. a and c
    e. b and c

20. Deviant labels may incline persons toward further deviation since:
    a. a deviant label limits legitimate occupational opportunities
    b. being labeled may increase illegitimate economic opportunities
    c. a deviant label can affect self-conceptions
    d. all of the above
    e. none of the above

Essay

1. A. Explain the theories of differential association, subcultural deviance, and structural strain. (knowledge)
   B. Discuss two criticisms or shortcomings of each of these theories. (comprehension)
   C. Integrate these theories into a more complete explanation of deviance. Use an example. (analysis)

2. A. Explain the labeling theory. (knowledge)
   B. Discuss one criticism or shortcoming of this theory. (comprehension)
   C. Using a fictitious example, apply labeling theory to explain continued deviation. (application)

3. Discuss two biological theories of deviance. Show how research findings did or did not support these theories.

4. Discuss control theory. Be certain to explain in detail the four types of bonds that exist between the group and the individual.

5. Explain Durkheim's concepts of anomie and moral communities, and discuss two research findings about moral and social integration and crime rates.

Answers

Completion

1. deviant behavior
2. importance, frequency
3. Cesare Lombroso
4. males
5. self-esteem
6. differential association
7. norms
8. structural strain
9. Merton
10. control
11. social bonds
12. attachments, investments
13. normlessness
14. social integration
15. social integration
16. intentional
17. labeled a deviant
18. impulsive
19. intentional
20. primary

Multiple Choice

1. d
2. e
3. a
4. e
5. c
6. b
7. c
8. d
9. b
10. e
11. a
12. e
13. c
14. a
15. d
16. d
17. b
18. b
19. a
20. d

CHAPTER EIGHT

Social Control

Overview

Chapter 8 begins with a discussion of social control. It briefly describes mechanisms of informal social control and highlights the research by Asch and Schachter on the effects of the group on the behavior of its members. It then discusses more formal mechanisms of control and efforts of prevention, highlighting the Cambridge-Somerville experiment on delinquency prevention. This chapter also considers Gibbs's theory of deterrence, related research findings, and efforts to reform and resocialize deviants, including the TARP experiment. An appraisal of the current effectiveness of informal and formal mechanisms of social control closes the chapter.

Capsule Summary

Collective efforts to **ensure conformity** are forms of **social control**. Most **social control** is **informal** and relies on **our internalization of the norms, attachments,** and **power of groups to encourage conformity** among their members. **Laboratory studies** such as **Asch's** famous "line experiments" and **Schachter's** study of **group reactions to nonconformity** have demonstrated empirically the power of groups to affect the behavior of their members.

When **informal** methods **fail to produce conformity** and the **deviance** is also **illegal** or there are **legal grounds** for **intervention**, more **formal** mechanisms such as **police, prisons,** and **mental hospitals** are used. Formal controls are attempted in three ways: to **prevent** deviance by removing opportunities for it to occur, to **deter** deviance through the threat of punishment, and to **reform** or **resocialize** deviants to discourage them from future deviance.

In order for a deviant act to occur, there must be an **opportunity** to commit it. Hence many programs, such as neighborhood block watches, seek to remove these opportunities. It has long been assumed that **delinquency** has its **roots** in **early socialization**. Numerous **intervention** programs such as the **Cambridge-Somerville experiment** attempted to stem this tide; however, such experiments failed to produce the desired results.

Deterrence is based on the premise that the threat of punishment will discourage deviation. Although this idea was initially rejected by social scientists, recent studies such as those conducted by **Gibbs, Phillips, Stack, Sherman and Berk,** and **Erhrlich** indicate that the threat of punishment may deter deviance provided the punishment is **perceived** as **swift, certain,** and **severe.** Indeed, the relative **ineffectiveness** of our current criminal justice system in **preventing deviance** may stem from the fact that **these three criteria are not often met.**

Much attention has been paid recently to the **therapeutic** function of prisons. Attempts have been made to **resocialize** and **reform prisoners** in the hope that they **would not return**

to crime on release. Again, studies such as the TARP experiment do not indicate any significant effect of these efforts, and **recidivism rates** remain high.

Although recent data may seem pessimistic, social control is effective in many cases. Actually, few people commit crimes, but for those few who do engage in serious deviation, the current criminal justice system has not proved to be very effective.

Key Concepts

You should be able to explain the concepts listed here; be prepared to supply several examples of each concept.

Social control 204

Informal social control 206

Internalization of norms 206

Formal social control 209

Deterrence 215

Penitentiary 226

Auburn prison model 227

Recidivism 227

Resocialization 227

Key Research Studies

Know both the methodology and the results of the following research studies.

Asch: study of group conformity 206

Schachter: group reactions to nonconformity 208

Cabot and others: delinquency prevention by socialization (Cambridge-Somerville experiment) 210

Gibbs and others: effects of punishment on deterrence 217

Sherman and Beck: deterring wife beating 218

Ehrlich and others: capital punishment and deterrence 220

Lenihan, Rossi, and Berk: financial support of released convicts and recidivism rates (TARP study) 228

Key Theories

Although attempts at prison reform are not theories in the typical sense, they are broader than concepts and do make assumptions, so they are included here.

Opportunity theory

Deterrence theory

Attempts at prison reform

Completion

1. All collective efforts to ensure conformity to the norms are forms of _____.

2. When _____ methods of control fail and more serious acts of deviance occur, _____ methods of social control are activated.

3. Activities by organizations created to ensure conformity to the norms are termed _____.

4. When norms become _____, they become a part of our own beliefs about how we should act.

5. In his famous "line experiments," Asch showed the influence of the group on _____.

6. Formal social control attempts to _____ and to reform or resocialize people.

7. Opportunity theory argues that in order for a crime to occur there must be people motivated to commit an offense, suitable targets, and a(n) _____.

8. The Cambridge-Somerville experiment found that the socialization program had _____ effect on delinquency.

9. The use of punishment to discourage people from deviance is termed _____.

10. Gibbs postulated that the more _____, the more certain and the more _____ the punishment for a crime, the lower the rate at which such a crime will occur.

11. It has been found that what matters is not the actual certainty, swiftness, or severity of punishment but the _____ of these aspects of punishment.

12. Sherman and Berk found that men who were arrested for wife beating were _____ likely to commit a new offense than those who were advised or ordered to leave.

13. Sherman and Berk's study of wife beating offered strong support for _____ theory.

14. Phillips argued that deterrence depends on how much _____ is given to executions.

15. Stack's data supported Phillips's results even though he controlled for both the proportion of the population in the age group 16–34 and the _____ rate.

16. About _____ as many crimes are committed as are reported.

17. In the 1800s and early 1900s most prisons were modeled after the _____ design.

18. The proportion of those released from prison who are sentenced to prison again is termed the _____.

19. Efforts to change a person's socialization—to socialize a person over again in hopes of getting him or her to conform to the norms—is termed _____.

20. Whether capital punishment works and whether it is morally justified are _____ questions.

Multiple Choice

1. Formal social control is attempted through:
   a. preventing deviance
   b. deterring deviance
   c. reforming deviants
   d. a and b
   e. all of the above

2. Asch's experiments found that:
   a. a high proportion of people will conform even in a weak situation
   b. a low proportion of people will conform even in a weak situation
   c. the smaller the group, the greater the influence of the group on conformity
   d. the larger the group, the greater the influence of the group on conformity
   e. a and d

3. Schachter's study of group conformity found that:
   a. when the paid deviants stuck to their position they began to receive less attention
   b. as soon as the paid deviants expressed their views they began to receive less attention
   c. group members tended to like the deviant as well as they liked the more conforming members of the group
   d. all of the above
   e. none of the above

4. Informal social control is attempted by:
   a. internalization of norms
   b. deterring deviance by threat of punishment
   c. reforming people
   d. b and c
   e. all of the above

5. Opportunity theory recognizes that, for a crime to occur, there must be:
   a. the presence of effective guardians
   b. suitable targets
   c. people motivated to commit an offense
   d. a and c
   e. b and c

6. The Cambridge-Somerville experiment found that:
   a. boys in the experimental group committed fewer delinquent acts than did boys in the control group
   b. boys in the experimental group committed more delinquent acts than did boys in the control group
   c. there was no difference in conviction rates between the experimental group and the control group
   d. the more publicity given an execution, the lower the homicide rate
   e. the smaller the group, the greater its influence on conformity

7. Experiments in the area of delinquency prevention have generally:
   a. been highly successful in preventing delinquency
   b. been failures in preventing delinquency
   c. succeeded in changing the life circumstances of the children
   d. a and c
   e. none of the above

8. Gibbs postulated that the more _____ the punishment for a crime, the lower the rate at which such a crime will occur:
   a. severe
   b. certain
   c. swift
   d. a and c
   e. all of the above

9. Gibbs's theory of deterrence:
   a. predicts that severe sentences will not effectively deter crimes if people realize that they have little chance of being caught
   b. can apply to all deviant acts
   c. was not supported by empirical research
   d. a and c
   e. all of the above

10. In their study of wife beating Sherman and Berk found that those men who had the highest rate of repeat offenses were those who had:
   a. been arrested
   b. been ordered to leave the premises
   c. been offered some advice and mediation
   d. been labeled deviant
   e. none of the above

11. The use of punishment to discourage people from committing deviance is termed:
   a. prevention
   b. deterrence
   c. resocialization
   d. revenge
   e. reform

12. Phillips's study of capital punishment as deterrence:
   a. found no evidence that capital punishment deters homicide
   b. the homicide rate is lower immediately following a well-publicized execution
   c. the deterrent effect depends on how much publicity an execution is given
   d. b and c
   e. none of the above

13. Stack's study of the impact of publicized executions on homicide rates:
   a. argued that since the data supported deterrence theory the author strongly supported capital punishment
   b. did not support deterrence theory and argued against capital punishment
   c. produced results that agreed with Phillips's
   d. a and c
   e. none of the above

14. Table 8-1 indicates that the most reported crime was:
   a. auto theft
   b. larceny
   c. rape
   d. purse snatching
   e. burglary

15. Table 8-2 indicates that the crime *most likely* to be solved is:
   a. assault
   b. rape
   c. robbery
   d. homicide
   e. a and b

16. Punishment for those who commit crimes in the United States is:
    a. very certain
    b. very swift
    c. very severe
    d. all of the above
    e. none of the above

17. The first to experiment with the use of a penitentiary was:
    a. the ancient Greeks under Plato
    b. the Quakers in Pennsylvania
    c. the British during the 1700s
    d. Cabot's Cambridge-Somerville experiment
    e. none of the above

18. Reform efforts in prison are probably hampered by:
    a. a further weakening of an inmate's attachments with conventional people
    b. the stigma associated with being an ex-convict, which hinders the formation of attachments with conventional people
    c. new attachments to other deviants made while in prison
    d. a and b
    e. all of the above

19. In the TARP experiment, the recidivism rate for the control group was _____ as the experimental group.
    a. much lower
    b. much higher
    c. slightly lower
    d. slightly higher
    e. the same

20. Which of the following statements is/are true?
    a. if crime can be reduced by overhauling the criminal justice system we could expect truly dramatic changes
    b. a great deal of our conformity is rooted in informal social control
    c. Social control does not appear to work since more than 13 million crimes are reported each year
    d. all of the above
    e. none of the above

Essay

1. A. Name the three criteria that must be present if punishment is to serve as a deterrent. (Gibbs) (knowledge)
   B. Explain Gibbs's theory of deterrence. (comprehension)
   C. What does Gibbs's theory imply about our current criminal justice system? (application)

2. A. Describe either Asch's or Schachter's study of group conformity. (comprehension)
   B. Show how these results might affect real world (rather than laboratory) social interaction. (application)
   C. Compare and contrast these studies in terms of methodology and results. (analysis)

3. Discuss the Cambridge-Somerville experiment. What do the results of this and other intervention programs imply about delinquency prevention?

4. Discuss the capital punishment controversy by examining the issues involved and recent research findings.

5. Briefly trace the history of prisons in the United States. Explain why contemporary prisons, for the most part, fail in their mission to reform inmates.

Answers

Completion

1. social control
2. informal, formal
3. formal methods of social control
4. internalized
5. an individual's conformity
6. prevent deviance
7. absence of effective guardians
8. no
9. deterrence
10. rapid, severe
11. perceptions
12. less
13. deterrence
14. publicity
15. unemployment
16. twice
17. Auburn
18. recidivism rate
19. resocialization
20. unrelated

Multiple Choice

1. e	11. b
2. a	12. d
3. a	13. c
4. a	14. a
5. e	15. d
6. c	16. e
7. b	17. b
8. e	18. e
9. a	19. e
10. c	20. b

Review and Special Project

Review

This unit discussed the relationship between the individual and the group, as well as the biological and cultural basis for behavior. It emphasized informal and formal social control and described the various theories of deviation. You may wish to apply your knowledge of this material to the following project.

Special Project

Conduct an interview with someone who has committed an act that would qualify as a serious deviance. This need not be an illegal act; it could be behavior that, if discovered, would have resulted in trouble with the police, school authorities, or employers. The subject need not have been caught. It will probably not be difficult to locate such a person. Remember that what may be conforming in one subculture may be deviant in the general culture.

Be certain to secure your subject's consent; explain to him or her the nature and purpose of your interview, and respect your subject's confidentiality by allowing your subject to remain anonymous if he or she asks to be unnamed.

During your interview try to obtain as much information as you can about the following:

1. The subject's situation at the time of the deviance: age, employment, family situation, personal problems, and so on.
2. The subject's background: education, religion, family, and social class.
3. The actual situation in which the deviant act occurred: alone or with others, spur of the moment or planned.
4. The purpose of the deviation: fun, material gain, the venting of anger, and so on.
5. Has the deviation been repeated? If so, why? If not, why not?
6. Was the subject caught? If so, what happened?

After your interview has been conducted, attempt to explain this deviation by using some of the theories you have studied. Focus on the mechanisms of social control that may or may not have been effective. Does this case seem to fit a particular theory, or does your explanation entail components of several theories? Do any theories fail to fit this case at all? Attempt to develop your own theory of deviance applicable to this situation.

CHAPTER NINE

Concepts and Theories of Stratification

Overview

This largely theoretical chapter describes modern social theories of stratification. It opens with a discussion of Marx's two-class model and then discusses Weber's three-dimensional approach to social class. It describes Lenski's theory of status inconsistency and cites related research findings. It distinguishes between ascribed and achieved statuses and differentiates between structural and exchange mobility. Chapter 9 then turns its attention to Marx's utopian classless society and Dahrendorf's critique of Marx. After Mosca's theory of the inevitability of stratification is summarized, the chapter turns its attention to the functionalist, social evolutionary, and conflict approaches to stratification. Throughout the discussion of these theoretical approaches, an example of a "toy society" illustrates the various concepts and assumptions. This chapter offers a more in-depth explanation of many of the concepts introduced in Chapter 2. Likewise it sets the stage for many of the chapters that follow.

Capsule Summary

Social stratification, the unequal distribution of rewards in a society, has long been the subject of considerable interest. Divisions of wealth and rank within societies are termed **social classes**.

Marx, who developed the first modern social theory of stratification, viewed class from the **economic dimension**. To Marx, class membership was based on one's relationship to the **means of production**. Those who own the means of production were termed **bourgeoisie**, and those who work it were termed **proletariat**. Class membership was defined by both one's **material position** in society and one's **class consciousness**. Marx was a **utopian** who argued for a **classless society** based on the **abolition** of **private property**. In his critique of Marx, **Dahrendorf** argued that communistic societies were only classless by definition. **Stratification** in these societies was based on **control** rather than ownership of the means of production.

Weber argued for a broader definition of class. To **Weber**, class membership was determined by three dimensions: **class** (also termed **property**), **status** (also called **prestige**), and **power**. People disproportionately high (or low) on one dimension are termed status inconsistent. Research has found that **status inconsistent** people may experience **psychological stress** and often **favor** politically liberal causes.

Status may be based on **achievement** or **ascription**. **Caste** systems rely predominately on **ascription**, whereas **industrialized** societies rely more heavily on **achievement**. Social mobility, which results from changes in the distribution of statuses, is termed **structural mobility**. Mobility that is not structural is termed **exchange mobility**.

Mosca argued that stratification is the **inevitable result** of **political organization**, which fosters **inequalities in power** and allows those with greater power to **exploit** others for **material advantage**.

The **functional, social evolutionary**, and **conflict theories differ** in their **assumptions**, yet all assume that **some degree of stratification** is **inevitable**. Functionalists argue that the stratification system ensures that **functionally important** positions will be **filled** because those occupying such positions will be highly rewarded. The concepts of **functional importance** and the **principle of replaceability** are central to the **functionalist explanation**. **Social evolutionists** argue that **cultural accumulation** results in a **division of labor** and **specialization**. This, in turn, leads to **stratification**. **Conflict theorists** argue that societies are **even more stratified** than necessary because those in **powerful positions** use their power to **exploit** the **less powerful**. **Labor unions** and **professions**, for example, use their power to control **replaceability** and ensure their own continuation of power.

Key Concepts

You should be able to explain the concepts listed here. You should also be able to cite several examples of each concept.

Social stratification 234
Social class 234
Bourgeoisie 236
Proletariat 236
Means of production 236
Lumpenproletariat 236
Class consciousness 237
False class consciousness 237
Class (property) 239
Status (prestige) 239
Power 240

Status characteristics 241
Status inconsistency 241
Social mobility 243
Caste system 245
Structural mobility 245
Exchange mobility 245
Anarchy 247
Utopian 247
Functional importance 250
Principle of replaceability 251

Key Research Studies

You should be familiar with both the methodology and the results of the tests of the theory of status inconsistency by the following researchers.

Gary Marx 241
Cohn 242
Jackson 242
Baltzell 242

Key Theories

Be prepared to explain the assumptions of these theories and, when applicable, cite related research findings.
   Marx: stratification
   Weber: stratification
   Lenski: status inconsistency theory
   Dahrendorf: critique of Marx
   Mosca: stratification
   Davis and Moore: functionalist viewpoint
   Evolutionary perspective
   Conflict perspective

Completion

1.   Upward or downward movement by individuals or groups within a stratification system is termed _____.

2.   Divisions of rank and wealth within societies are termed _____.

3.   Marx termed the class of people who work the means of production the _____.

4.   Marx termed the very bottom of society's stratification system the _____.

5.   Marx termed the tendency for workers to believe they had common interests with the ruling class _____.

6.   Marx's definition of class is determined only by the _____ dimension.

7. Weber termed the three dimensions of stratification _____, _____, and _____.

8.   Weber considered groups of people with similar life chances as determined by their economic position in societal _____.

9.   The ability to get one's way despite the resistence of others is _____.

10. Modern social scientists consider the "Three P's" of stratification to be _____, _____, and _____.

11. Certain individual or group traits that determine status are termed _____.

12. Persons or groups who hold different ranks on each of the three dimensions are termed _____.

13. Jackson hypothesized that _____ can have mental health consequences.

14. _____ status is based on merit, whereas _____ status is a position based on who you are.

15. Social mobility that results from changes in the distribution of statuses in society is called _____.

16. A _____ constructs plans for an ideal society.

17. _____ argued that stratification cannot be avoided since it is an inescapable feature of collective life.

18. A position is of high functional importance to a society to the degree that either the _____ or its _____ are hard to replace.

19. _____ theories focus on how stratification systems are subject to distortion.

20. _____ argue that the accumulation of culture inevitably leads to a division of labor and therefore to stratification.

Multiple Choice

1. Marx termed those who work the means of production:
    a. the bourgeoisie
    b. the proletariat
    c. the lumpenproletariat
    d. the middle class
    e. none of the above

2. Which of the following groups was not incorporated into Marx's class system?
    a. the owners of the means of production
    b. farmers and peasants
    c. lumpenproletariat
    d. b and c
    e. all of the above

3. Marx defined the two classes on the basis of:
    a. their material position in society
    b. prestige
    c. power
    d. a and c
    e. all of the above

4. What Weber called class, modern social scientists refer to as:
   a. prestige
   b. status
   c. property
   d. power
   e. none of the above

5. The ability to get one's way despite the resistance of others is termed:
   a. property
   b. class
   c. power
   d. prestige
   e. none of the above

6. When famous sports stars endorse a commercial product they are exchanging their _____ for economic advantage.
   a. property
   b. prestige
   c. power
   d. class
   e. position

7. Which of the following would be *most* likely to experience status inconsistency?
   a. a white male lawyer
   b. a black engineer with a doctorate
   c. a female physician
   d. b and c
   e. a and c

8. Research in the area of status inconsistency had found that:
   a. upper-status blacks are more radical that lower-status blacks
   b. Jewish bankers and industrialists have a record of voting for conservative parties
   c. wealthy and powerful American Catholics have a strong preference for the Republican party
   d. all of the above
   e. none of the above

9. Jackson measured status inconsistency on the basis of:
   a. occupation
   b. education
   c. racial-ethnic background
   d. a and b
   e. all of the above

10. Jackson's data found:
    a. status inconsistency can have mental health consequences
    b. different patterns of inconsistency had different outcomes
    c. people of high status backgrounds with low status jobs had a high affinity for liberal politics and blamed the system for their failures
    d. a and b
    e. all of the above

11. When a society uses ascriptive status rules, people may be placed in status positions based on:
    a. place of birth
    b. family background
    c. sex
    d. b and c
    e. all of the above

12. In a caste system:
    a. status is based entirely on ascription
    b. ascription is the overwhelming basis for status
    c. status is based entirely on achievement
    d. achievement is the overwhelming basis for status
    e. none of the above

13. Exchange mobility:
    a. is common when the ascriptive status rule operates
    b. is very uncommon when status is based on achievement
    c. is very common regardless of the rules governing status
    d. a and b
    e. none of the above

14. Marx argued that in order to achieve a classless society:
    a. the proletariat should own the means of production
    b. the state should be abolished
    c. private ownership of the means of production should be abolished
    d. the bourgeoisie should own the means of production
    e. none of the above

15. Mosca argued that:
    a. human societies cannot exist without political organization
    b. whenever there is political organization there must be inequalities in power
    c. a classless society is possible if private ownership is abolished
    d. a and b
    e. b and c

16. The functionalist view of stratification argues that:
    a. positions in society differ in the degree to which they are functionally important
    b. some positions are inherently more difficult to fill than others
    c. to ensure an adequate supply of people to fill important positions it is necessary to attach higher rewards to those positions
    d. all of the above
    e. none of the above

17. Which of the following theorists is/are correctly paired with his view or theory of stratification?
    a. Lenski—social evolutionary
    b. Davis and Moore—conflict
    c. Marx—functionalist theory
    d. all of the above
    e. none of the above

18. A position is of high functional importance when:
    a. the position itself is hard to replace
    b. the occupants of the position are hard to replace
    c. its functions can be performed by people in other positions
    d. a and b
    e. all of the above

19. _____ theory takes the premise that the accumulation of culture results in cultural specialization, which in turn results in stratification.
    a. functionalist
    b. social evolutionary
    c. conflict
    d. Marxist
    e. Weberian

20. Most modern conflict theorists:
    a. argue that stratification is unavoidable
    b. assume that people who are in a position to exploit others will do so
    c. argue that societies are more stratified than necessary
    d. b and c
    e. all of the above

Essays

1. A. List the three theories of stratification. (knowledge)
    B. Explain the three theories of stratification. (comprehension)
    C. Compare and contrast two of these theories. (analysis)

2. A. Define the principle of replaceability. (knowledge)
   B. Give examples of the politics of replaceability from labor unions and the professions. (comprehension)
   C. Apply this principle to the "toy society." (application)

3. Contrast Marx and Weber on the subject of social class.

4. Discuss the concept of status inconsistency. Cite some research findings on this topic.

5. Discuss Marx on the classless society and explain Dahrendorf's critique.

Answers

Completion
1. social mobility
2. social classes
3. proletariat
4. lumpenproletariat
5. false consciousness
6. economic
7. class, status, power
8. classes
9. power
10. property, prestige, power
11. status characteristics
12. status inconsistent
13. status inconsistency
14. achieved, ascribed
15. structural mobility
16. utopian
17. Mosca
18. position itself, occupants
19. conflict
20. evolutionary theories

Multiple Choice
1. b
2. d
3. a
4. c
5. c
6. b
7. d
8. a
9. e
10. d
11. e
12. b
13. e
14. c
15. d
16. d
17. a
18. d
19. b
20. e

CHAPTER TEN

Comparing Systems of Stratification

Overview

This chapter contrasts the stratification systems of hunting and gathering, agrarian, and industrialized societies. It starts with a description of hunting and gathering societies and then describes the changes brought about by the advent of agrarian societies. It also describes the stratification systems of agrarian societies and examines the differences between the elite and the masses. Chapter 10 then discusses the changes in the stratification system brought about by industrialization, focusing on research findings about mobility in industrialized nations. The chapter closes with a special topic on the aspects of income inequalities in America. Many of the concepts first introduced in Chapters 2 and 9 are applied to the various stratification systems.

Capsule Summary

Stratification exists in all societies, even the simplest **hunting and gathering societies** composed of **small bands of people who wander in search of food.** They are the **least stratified** of all societies and have **few possessions, no full-time leaders,** and little **role specialization.** Stratification is typically based on **age** and **sex,** although **within the sexes** it is often based on **achieved characteristics.**

As societies became **more complex** they became **more stratified. Agrarian societies** fostered the rise of **specialization, personal property, government, cities,** and **slavery.** These societies were **highly stratified** with **large gaps** separating the **elite** from the **masses. Agrarian** societies were **dominated** by the **military** and were often in a **chronic state of warfare.**

Industrialization changed the stratification system. Societies became **less stratified.** The gap between the **top** and **bottom decreased** as the **middle classes** expanded and jobs for unskilled labor began to disappear. As **more skill** and **training** were required for jobs, **positions** and **their occupants** became **less replaceable;** workers thus became **more powerful** and **better able to resist coercion.** The rise of **democracy** and **industrialization** went hand in hand.

Research has found **high rates of structural mobility** in **industrialized nations.** Compared with European nations, the United States has higher rates of **long-distance mobility.** Recent research by **Blau and Duncan, Porter,** and **Cohen and Tyree** has focused on **status attainment** in the United States and Canada and the application of the **status attainment model** to mobility in these nations. The results of research have yielded some surprising results. Whereas earlier studies of mobility focused only upon the male, more recent studies have also focused on **female mobility** and **status attainment.**

Key Concepts

You should be able to explain the following concepts; be prepared to provide several examples of each concept.

Hunting and gathering society 259

Agrarian society 263

Specialization 263

Industrialization 270

Industrial society 270

Structural mobility 273

Long-distance mobility 274

Status attainment model 275

Key Research Studies

Be familiar with both the methodology and the results of the research studies cited here.

Lipset and Bendix: comparative social mobility 273

Sewell: longitudinal study of mobility of high school graduates

Blau and Duncan: comparison of rates of long-distance mobility 275

Blau and Duncan: status attainment model 275

Cohen and Tyree: comparison of mobility of those from poor versus nonpoor backgrounds 276

Porter et al.: status attainment in Canada 276

Aspects of Income Inequalities in America (Special Topic 2) 280

Key Theories

You should be able to explain the assumptions of these theories as they apply to stratification in industrial societies; when applicable, cite related research findings.

Functionalism

Conflict theory

In addition to these theories, you should be *thoroughly* familiar with stratification systems of:

Hunting and gathering societies

Agrarian societies

Industrial societies

Completion

1. The simplest type of society is the _____ society.

2. Recent archeological discoveries in Africa indicate that humans existed more than _____ ago.

3. The primary basis for stratification in hunting and gathering societies is age and _____.

4. Within age and sex groups simple societies are not very _____.

5. With the invention of plows and effective animal harnesses, _____ societies appeared.

6. The advent of agriculture made possible _____ and _____.

7. _____ societies lived in a chronic state of warfare.

8. Because agrarian societies were based on _____, they tended to be expansionistic.

9. The most stratified societies are typically _____ societies.

10. Industrial societies are not based on getting people to work harder but to _____.

11. Using technology to make work much more productive is termed _____.

12. As positions become _____ replaceable, their relative rewards increase.

13. As a consequence of industrialization, the average worker is more _____ and thus more able to resist coercion.

14. Compared to agrarian societies, industrial societies are _____ stratified.

15. Bendix and Lipset observed that in industrial societies there is a great deal of _____ mobility.

16. _____ mobility involves high upward or downward shifts in status.

17. Blau and Duncan found a very strong correlation between _____ and occupational status.

18. Studies of status attainment in Canada have found that it is very _____ to that of the United States.

19. Cohen and Tyree have found the main determinant of the family income of persons from all backgrounds is _____.

20.* _____ interests play a consistent and marked role in political behavior and attitudes.

*Note: Question 20 is drawn from Special Topic 2.

Multiple Choice

1. The simplest form of society is the _____ society.
   a. gardening
   b. hunting and gathering
   c. agrarian
   d. industrial
   e. herding

2. The least stratified societies are:
   a. agrarian societies
   b. hunting and gathering societies
   c. industrialized societies
   d. herding societies
   e. horticultural societies

3. In a hunting and gathering society:
   a. there is extensive role specialization
   b. power is based on land ownership
   c. stratification is generally based on sex and age
   d. a and c
   e. all of the above

4. The rule seems to be the _____ a human society is, the less it is stratified.
   a. smaller
   b. poorer
   c. more secure
   d. a and b
   e. all of the above

5. Improved agriculture produced:
   a. warfare
   b. cities
   c. surplus
   d. b and c
   e. all of the above

6. Slavery is most likely to be found in:
   a. hunting and gathering societies
   b. agrarian societies
   c. industrialized societies
   d. a and b
   e. all of the above

7. The ability to produce surplus food may lead to:
   a. humans becoming property
   b. a more extensive division of labor
   c. government
   d. all of the above
   e. none of the above

8. In an agrarian society the masses and the elite may differ in:
   a. language
   b. ethnic background
   c. the amount of time devoted to leisure activities
   d. a and c
   e. all of the above

9. The most highly stratified societies tend to be:
   a. agrarian
   b. herding
   c. gardening
   d. industrialized
   e. b and c

10. Changes in the stratification system brought about by industrialization include:
    a. a widening of the gap between the masses and the elite
    b. positions become more replaceable
    c. a decrease in the power of the average worker, who is less able to resist coercion
    d. all of the above
    e. none of the above

11. Which of the following statements is/are true?
    a. as positions become less replaceable, their relative rewards decrease
    b. to the extent that occupational positions require education and training they are less replaceable
    c. in the long run industrialization has made the average worker more replaceable
    d. a and c
    e. all of the above

12. Consequences of industrialization include:
    a. people "work smarter"
    b. the average worker has become less replaceable
    c. the training necessary to do most jobs has enabled workers to demand a higher level of reward
    d. all of the above
    e. none of the above

13. Differences between industrialized and agrarian societies include:
    a. industrial societies are more stratified
    b. industrial societies are less stratified
    c. the gap between the poor and the wealthy is greater in an industrial society
    d. a and c
    e. b and c

14. Cohen and Tyree found:
    a. education has less importance for status attainment for people from poor homes than for other people
    b. education has greater importance for status attainment for people from poor homes than for other homes
    c. the main determinant of the family income of persons from all backgrounds is marital status
    d. a and c
    e. b and c

15. Huge upward and downward shifts in status are termed _____ mobility.
    a. exchange
    b. structural
    c. long-distance
    d. vertical
    e. horizontal

16. Blau and Duncan ("status attainment model") found:
    a. it's better to start at the top than at the bottom of the stratification system
    b. the primary mechanism linking the occupational status of fathers and sons is education
    c. family background is a more important influence on status attainment than is education
    d. a and b
    e. a and c

17. Studies of status attainment in Canada have found:
    a. Canada's rate of social mobility is almost identical to that of the United States
    b. opportunities for occupational advancement in Canada were much more restricted than in most industrialized nations
    c. ethnicity plays a major role in status attainment
    d. all of the above
    e. b and c

18. Studies of female status attainment in Canada have shown:
  a. native-born Canadian women with full-time jobs come from lower-status family backgrounds than do their male counterparts
  b. the average native-born Canadian woman has a higher status occupation than do similar males
  c. the correlations between women's occupational prestige and their fathers' occupational prestige are much lower than for men
  d. b and c
  e. all of the above

19.* Which of the following is/are true about income inequalities in America?
  a. people are not very aware of their relative position in the stratification system
  b. a majority of Americans identify themselves as lower class
  c. employed Americans are amazingly satisfied with their jobs at all levels of income
  d. all of the above
  e. none of the above

20.* Which of the following is/are true about the relationship between social class and life-style?
  a. the proportion of people who drink alcoholic beverages decreases with income
  b. lower-income people are less likely to read a newspaper daily than upper-income people
  c. lower-income people are less likely to socialize with relatives than are upper-income people
  d. a and b
  e. all of the above

*Note: Questions 19 and 20 are drawn from Special Topic 2.

Essays

1. A. List the three types of societies. (knowledge)
    B. Explain the stratification systems in each of these societies. (comprehension)
    C. Contrast the stratification systems of hunting and gathering societies with those of agrarian societies. (analysis)

2. A. Explain the stratification systems in agrarian and industrialized societies. (comprehension)
    B. Show how industrialization changed the stratification system. (application)
    C. Contrast the stratification systems of these two societies. (analysis)

3. Discuss some of the research findings on social mobility.

4. Explain the statement "The smaller, the poorer, and the less secure society is, the less it is stratified."

5. Discuss five research findings about the relationship between social class and life-style as these were described in Special Topic 2, Aspects of Income Inequalities in America.

Answers

Completion
1. hunting and gathering
2. 3 million years
3. sex
4. stratified
5. agrarian
6. specialization, cities
7. agrarian
8. military rule
9. agrarian
10. work smarter
11. industrialization
12. less
13. powerful
14. less
15. structural
16. long distance
17. education
18. similar
19. marital status
20. class

Multiple Choice
1. b
2. b
3. c
4. d
5. e
6. b
7. d
8. e
9. a
10. e
11. b
12. d
13. b
14. e
15. c
16. d
17. a
18. d
19. c
20. b

CHAPTER ELEVEN

Intergroup Conflict: Racial and Ethnic Inequality

Overview

Chapter 11 opens with a discussion of intergroup conflict and mechanisms for reducing these conflicts. It explains early theories such as authoritarianism, which argues that conflict results from prejudice. Then it focuses on more recent explanations such as Allport's contact theory, which argues that prejudice results from social inequality and competition. Using examples, the chapter shows how inequality and economic competition may lead to prejudice. This chapter also turns its attention to slavery and its aftermath and discusses Myrdal's *The American Dilemma*. The decline of prejudice is then discussed with examples such as the case of Japanese immigrants in the United States and Canada. The chapter also considers today's minorities and analyzes their plight and recent progess from the perspective of "new immigrants." The chapter closes with a discussion of the importance of enclave economies, integration patterns, and barriers to black progress. A special topic that focuses on minority participation in sports and entertainment as a mechanism for overcoming discrimination is included at the end.

Capsule Summary

Prejudice is often the result of **intergroup conflict** and **status inequality**. **Intergroup conflict** may include both **racial** and **ethnic groups**. This conflict may be resolved through **assimilation, accommodation** (and hence **pluralism**), **extermination** or **expulsion** of the weaker group, or the **imposition** of a **caste system**. Earlier theories such as the **authoritarian personality theory** argued that prejudice **caused intergroup conflict**. More recent theories argue that the reverse is correct.

Allport's contact theory argues that contact between groups will **reduce prejudice** if the two groups meet on the **basis** of **equal status** and **pursue common goals**. Research has supported this claim. Conditions imposed by slavery and its aftermath (sometimes termed "the **American dilemma**") illustrate the reverse of this theory. **Inequality, economic competition**, and the **imposition of a caste system** can **increase prejudice**. Minorities do not always occupy the lowest status. **Middleman minorities** frequently are a buffer between the highest and lowest classes and are often the targets of their frustration.

Historically, many minorities have achieved **upward mobility** through the **mechanisms** of **geographic concentration, internal economic development**, and **occupational specialization** and through the development of a **middle class** and the creation of **enclave economies. Japanese Americans** and **Japanese Canadians** are prime examples.

Today's minorities—blacks, Native Americans, and **Chicanos**, for example—**differ** from other minorities in that they have **resided** in the **United States** and **Canada** for **many generations**. Still they have been treated almost as a **caste apart** from **mainstream society**.

For this reason many sociologists view them as recent immigrants and analyze their recent progress from that standpoint. Until recently **blacks**, for example, have been concentrated in the **rural South** where they received **little education** or **training necessary** for **upward mobility** in an **urban, industrialized society**. They have been further **hampered** by their **visibility, large population, lack of a "homeland,"** and the **legacies of slavery**. Prejudice still exists, although recent **gains** made by these minorities are reflected in **integration** patterns in **residence** and **church attendance**.

Key Concepts

You should be able to explain the concepts listed here, as well as cite several examples of each concept.

Intergroup conflict 292	Prejudice 295
Race 293	Authoritarian 295
Ethnic group 293	Exclusion 306
Assimilation 294	Cultural division of labor 308
Accommodation 294	Middleman minorities 308
Extermination 294	Enclave economy 318
Cultural (ethnic) pluralism 294	Visibility 326
Segregation 294	

Key Research Studies

Be familiar with both the methodology and the results of the following research studies.
Various studies of the relationship between prejudice and other variables 295
Sherif and Sherif: artificial inducement of prejudice 296
Stark from N.O.R.C.: integration patterns in residence and church attendance 324

Key Figures

You should be able to associate each person with his contribution.
Charles Darwin: *biological* theory of evolution
Gunnar Myrdal: *An American Dilemma*
Gordon Allport: *The Nature of Prejudice*

Key Theories

Be prepared to explain the assumptions of these theories and, when applicable, cite related research findings. Blalock's theory appears in Special Topic 3.
    Theories of prejudice: authoritarian personality; contact theory; status inequality
    Bonaduch's model: labor and minorities
    Three mechanisms that foster upward mobility
    Enclave Economy Theory
    Blacks as recent immigrants
    Blalock's explanation of minorities' success in sports

In addition, you should be *thoroughly* familiar with the experiences of the various minorities discussed in this chapter.

Completion

1. A human group with some observable common biological feature is termed a _____.

2. Ethnic groups are groups whose _____ differ.

3. For a long time it was believed that intergroup conflicts in North America would be resolved through _____.

4. When intergroup conflict ends through _____ the result is ethnic or cultural pluralism.

5. Besides accommodation and assimilation, the possible outcomes of intergroup conflict include _____, _____, and _____.

6. Until very recently, most social scientists regarded _____ as the cause of intergroup conflict.

7. Adorno argued that prejudice was the result of a(n) _____ personality type.

8. Contact theory is most closely associated with _____.

9. Allport argued that prejudice will _____ if two groups are engaged in competition.

10. The more highly _____ a person is and the higher a person's _____, the less likely a person is to be prejudiced against other racial and ethnic groups.

11. Myrdal's *An American Dilemma* dealt with the contradiction between _____ and _____.

12. There is no greater status inequality than that between _____ and _____.

13. Lieberson concluded that fear of blacks as _____ is the real cause of racial stereotypes.

14. According to Bonaduch, factors that lead subordinate groups to work for substandard wages include a low standard of living, a lack of political power, _____ and _____.

15. A minority that serves as both a link and a buffer between the upper and lower classes is referred to as a _____ minority.

16. Sociologists today consider the experience of blacks in America to be similar to that of _____.

17. When racial or ethnic groups tend to specialize in a few occupations, it is termed a(n) _____.

18. The degree to which a racial or ethnic group can be recognized is termed _____.

19. _____ theory proposes that the spatial concentration of an ethnic group permits them to create their own business enterprises, thus speeding the economic progress of the group.

20. Barriers to black progress include the legacies of slavery, visibility, and _____.

Multiple Choice

1. Races may differ on the basis of:
   a. skin color
   b. eyelid shape
   c. blood type
   d. a and b
   e. all of the above

2. Possible outcomes of intergroup conflict include:
   a. accommodation
   b. expulsion of the weaker group
   c. the imposition of a caste system
   d. a and b
   e. all of the above

3. Ethnic groups are:
   a. groups whose cultural heritage differs from other groups within the same society
   b. "involuntary" groups since people don't choose to join them
   c. groups that share observable biological differences
   d. a and b
   e. a and c

4. When intergroup conflict ends through accommodation, the result is:
   a. ethnic or cultural pluralism
   b. assimilation
   c. expulsion of the weaker group
   d. all of the above
   e. none of the above

5. The theory that some people are so oversocialized that they accept only their group's norms and values argues that prejudice is the result of:
   a. intergroup conflict
   b. status inequality
   c. competitive contact with others
   d. the authoritarian personality
   e. none of the above

6. Contact theory is most closely associated with:
   a. Gordon Allport
   b. Gunnar Myrdal
   c. Thomas Sowell
   d. H. M. Blalock
   e. none of the above

7. According to contact theory, prejudice will intensify when:
   a. the groups possess equal status in the situation
   b. cooperate to pursue common goals
   c. are engaged in competition
   d. a and b
   e. all of the above

8. *The American Dilemma* was written by:
   a. Gordon Allport
   b. Gunnar Myrdal
   c. Muzafer Sherif
   d. Thomas Sowell
   e. H. M. Blalock

9. Today most sociologists view status inequality as:
   a. the cause of prejudice but the result of discrimination
   b. the cause of, not the result of, prejudice and discrimination
   c. the result of prejudice and discrimination
   d. the cause of discrimination and the result of prejudice
   e. none of the above

10. Lieberson believes that the real cause of racial stereotypes is:
   a. fear of black and white intermarriage
   b. differences in skin color
   c. prejudice and discrimination
   d. fear of blacks as economic competitors
   e. none of the above

11. Bonaduch argued that factors that often cause or require members of subordinate groups to work for substandard wages include:
   a. a low standard of living
   b. a lack of information
   c. a lack of political power
   d. all of the above
   e. a and c

12. Strategies used to prevent a subordinate group from competing with the dominate group economically include:
   a. exclusion
   b. the establishment of a caste system
   c. accommodation
   d. a and b
   e. all of the above

13. Middleman minorities:
   a. may serve as a link between the upper and lower classes
   b. may serve as a buffer between the upper and lower classes
   c. may defuse potential class conflicts by becoming the focus of frustration and anger
   d. b and c
   e. all of the above

14. The typical occupation for first-generation Japanese Americans and Canadians is:
   a. farming and gardening
   b. mining
   c. garment work
   d. jewelry making
   e. none of the above

15. Mechanisms by which minorities have achieved upward mobility include:
    a. occupational generalization
    b. geographical concentration
    c. the development of a middle class
    d. b and c
    e. all of the above

16. Internal economic development by minorities is often enhanced by:
    a. the founding of their own financial institutions
    b. the development of an enclave economy
    c. buying outside of their own community
    d. a and b
    e. all of the above

17. Until very recently blacks in the United States:
    a. lived predominately in the South
    b. lived mainly in urban areas
    c. had a low level of education
    d. a and c
    e. all of the above

18. Barriers to black progress and upward mobility include:
    a. the legacies of slavery
    b. the lack of a "homeland"
    c. their visibility
    d. all of the above
    e. none of the above

19. According to the data on integration from the National Opinion Reseach Center:
    a. southern whites are very likely to live on the same block as blacks
    b. southern whites very rarely live on the same block as blacks
    c. blacks and whites are most likely to attend integrated churches in the South
    d. all of the above
    e. none of the above

20. When racial equality has been achieved:
    a. all members of each group must be of the same status
    b. the distribution of their members in the social structure is the same
    c. a person's race does not reliably indicate his or her status
    d. b and c
    e. a and b

Essay

1. A. Name three ways in which intergroup conflict may be resolved. (knowledge)
    B. Explain Allport's contact theory. (comprehension)
    C. Apply Allport's theory to a fictitious situation in a school or work setting. (application)

2. A. Name three ways in which minorities may achieve upward mobility. (knowledge)
    B. Explain economic enclave theory. (comprehension)
    C. Do the experiences of black Americans seem to support or negate this theory? Explain. (application)

3. Using an example, show how economic inequalities and status differences can lead to prejudice.

4. Trace the experiences of Japanese-Americans from their initial arrival in America to their position in American society today. Be certain to integrate into your explanation the various mechanisms by which minorities may achieve upward mobility.

5. Trace the experiences of blacks in America from slavery to the present. Show how their position may be likened to that of recent immigrants.

Answers

Completion
1. race
2. cultural heritages
3. assimilation
4. accommodation
5. extermination, expulsion, the imposition of a caste
6. prejudice
7. authoritarian
8. Gordon Allport
9. intensify
10. educated, income
11. democratic ideals, racist practices
12. master, slave
13. economic competitors
14. a lack of information, economic motives
15. middleman
16. recent immigrants
17. cultural division of labor
18. visibility
19. enclave economy
20. no homeland, numbers

Multiple Choice

1. e	11. d
2. e	12. d
3. d	13. e
4. a	14. a
5. d	15. d
6. a	16. d
7. c	17. d
8. b	18. d
9. b	19. b
10. d	20. d

CHAPTER TWELVE

Gender and Inequality

Overview

This chapter focuses on an analysis of gender and inequality using Guttentag and Secord's theory of sex ratios and sex roles. Many of the concepts introduced in earlier chapters are reviewed and applied to this analysis. Data from both Guttentag and Secord's study and from the author's analysis of data from the National Opinion Resource Center is provided throughout.

The chapter opens with a discussion of this theory and offers reasons for imbalanced sex ratios. It then applies this theory to the historical cases of Athens and Sparta. The concepts of dyadic power and structural power are then discussed and integrated into a more complete sociological explanation. The chapter then turns its attention to trends in North American sex ratios and moves to a discussion of the "woman movement" and the rise of feminism. It then discusses women in the labor force and changing sexual norms. The chapter closes with an analysis of the impact of imbalanced sex ratios on the black family. Throughout the chapter the reader gets a true "over-the-shoulder" view of theory construction and research in action.

Capsule Summary

Sex ratios, the number of males per one hundred females, both affect and are affected by **characteristics** of the **social structure**. **Guttentag** and **Secord** argue that **sex roles** and **relationships** are strongly influenced by the ratio of males to females. Causes of **imbalanced sex ratios** include: **geographic mobility, female infanticide, health and diet, differential life expectancy, war,** and **sexual practices**. In those societies where there is an **excess of males, female status** tends to be **low, women** are **less likely** to be **employed outside the home**, the **divorce rate** is **low**, and the **birth rate** is **high**. Historically, in such societies, (for example, ancient Athens) women are considered the **property of men**, and **strict sexual norms restrict women's sexual conduct**. Conversely, in societies where **females outnumber males** (our own, for example), **sexual norms** are **relaxed, women are often employed outside the home,** and women often unite to form social movements.

Dyadic power refers to the capacity of each member of a dyad to impose his or her will on the other. An unfavorable sex ratio causes the member of the sex in **excess supply** to be in a position of **power dependency**. **Structural power** also plays a role in determining sex ratios and sex roles. In cases where males have lacked **dyadic power**, they have strengthened their **structural power**, imposing norms that severely restrict the freedom of women. In cases where an **excess of females** has caused males to have **dyadic power**, they have combined this with **structural power** to exploit women to the fullest.

Guttentag and Secord argue that when one gender faces a lack of **dyadic power** they will organize to remedy their problem. The **woman movement** and the rise of **feminism** in the nineteenth and twentieth centuries is an example of this.

Today, because **women outnumber men**, they **increasingly work outside the home**. **Two-earner households** are common, and **occupations** are **less gender segregated**. Still there is a **gender gap** in many fields. Men continue to earn higher wages, and many occupations (especially the high-paying ones) are still dominated by men. **Job turnover rates** are **higher for women**, and **sex role socialization** continues to play a role in limiting women's options.

The imbalanced sex ratio strongly affects today's **black family**. Contrary to popular opinion, the **black family** was quite **stable** until very recently. Today, however, black men are in short supply. The **illegitimacy ratio has increased**, black males **seem less willing** to **make commitments** on the **basis of sex**, and the number of **single-parent families headed by women** has risen markedly. These trends support the relationship between **sex ratios** and **sex roles** as postulated by **Guttentag** and **Secord**.

Key Concepts

You should be able to explain the concepts listed here. You should be able to cite several examples of each concept.

Sex ratio   336
Female infanticide   340
Dyadic power   345
Structural power   346
Feminism   352
Illegitimacy ratio   366

Key Theory

You should be able to explain the assumptions of this theory and be able to cite related research findings.

Guttentag and Secord: sex ratios and sex roles

You should also be familiar with the data the author provides from the N.O.R.C. social survey.

Completion

1.   The number of males per one hundred females is termed the _____.

2.   In nations where men outnumber women, female status tends to be _____.

3. Where men outnumber women, the divorce rate is _____, and the birth rate is _____.

4. The major cause of imbalanced sex ratios is _____.

5. Where women are in excess, there is much _____ gender inequality.

6. _____ have higher fetal deaths and infant and childhood mortality rates.

7. Imbalanced sex ratios may be caused by geographic mobility, female infanticide, health and diet, war, _____, and _____.

8. Ancient Sparta is an example of a society where _____ outnumber _____.

9. _____ refers to the capacity of each member of a dyad to impose his or her will on the other member.

10. Power based on statuses within social structures is termed _____.

11. The individual member whose sex is in short supply has a _____ position and is _____ dependent on the partner because of the larger number of alternative relationships available.

12. When both _____ and dyadic power favor men, they respond by exploiting their advantage to the fullest.

13. In most societies women tend to marry men somewhat _____ than themselves.

14. When one gender group faces a substantial lack of _____ for an appreciable time, they will organize to seek ways to remedy their problem.

15. When men are in _____ supply, women increasingly find the need to become self-supporting.

16. Although the majority of women now work outside the home, they bring home significantly _____ money than men do.

17. Because female employment rates have risen rapidly, the average working woman is considerably _____ than the average working man.

18. The percentage of all births that occur out of wedlock is termed the _____.

19. Blacks have a substantially _____ infant mortality rate than whites.

20. The _____ movement was dedicated to obtaining the right to vote for all American women.

Multiple Choice

1. In nations where men outnumber women:
   a. women are less likely to be employed outside the home
   b. the divorce rate is high
   c. the birth rate is low
   d. b and c
   e. all of the above

2. Imbalanced sex ratios may be caused by:
   a. geographic mobility
   b. differential life expectancy
   c. sexual practices
   d. a and b
   e. all of the above

3. Female infanticide:
   a. has rarely been practiced in non-Western societies
   b. is the major cause of imbalanced sex ratios
   c. has been unknown in Europe since 1500
   d. b and c
   e. none of the above

4. Compared with females, males:
   a. have higher infant mortality rates
   b. have a lower rate of fetal deaths
   c. have lower childhood mortality rates
   d. b and c
   e. none of the above

5. Today, in most societies:
   a. men outlive women
   b. women outlive men
   c. men and women have about the same life expectancy
   d. most men over the age of 65 are widowed
   e. a and d

6. Athenian sexual practices included:
   a. isolation of "respectable" women by extremely protective sexual norms
   b. the highly visible presence of "disreputable" women
   c. male homosexuality
   d. all of the above
   e. none of the above

7. Characteristics of Spartan society included:
   a. girls were offered as much education as boys
   b. female infanticide was practiced, but male infanticide was unknown
   c. a Spartan wife was considered her husband's property
   d. b and c
   e. none of the above

8. The capacity of each member of a dyad to impose his or her will on the other member is termed:
   a. structural power
   b. dyadic power
   c. dyadic advantage
   d. structural advantage
   e. none of the above

9. Dependent members of dyadic relatives may seek to improve their bargaining positions by:
   a. developing cultural means to make themselves unusually attractive to the opposite sex
   b. spending more time in same-sex dyads
   c. withdrawing from dyadic relationships
   d. a and c
   e. all of the above

10. Men respond by exploiting their advantages to the fullest when:
   a. both structural and dyadic power favor women
   b. structural power favors men, but dyadic power favors women
   c. both structural and dyadic power favor men
   d. dyadic power favors men, but structural power favors women
   e. none of the above

11. The woman movement in the nineteenth and early twentieth centuries began and achieved its greatest prominance in the _____ states.
   a. midwestern
   b. northeastern
   c. southern
   d. western
   e. none of the above

12. Features of the feminist ideology include:
    a. opposition to all forms of stratification based on gender
    b. the belief that biology consigns females to inferior status
    c. a sense of common purpose among women to direct their efforts to bring about change
    d. a and c
    e. all of the above

13. Feminism:
    a. declined after the 1920s until the 1960s
    b. began in the 1960s
    c. sprang from the woman movement and the suffrage movement in the second decade of the twentieth century
    d. a and c
    e. all of the above

14. Changes resulting from the increased participation of women in the labor force include:
    a. occupations have become less gender segregated than they were in the past
    b. gender segregation of occupations has disappeared
    c. women bring home significantly less money than men
    d. a and c
    e. all of the above

15. Aspects of the gender wage gap include:
    a. women change jobs less often than do men
    b. the average working woman is considerably older than the average working man
    c. women take time out from the labor market more often than do men
    d. all of the above
    e. none of the above

16. Sex role socialization affects the gender gap since:
    a. women are more likely to be selected as leaders
    b. women are less likely to enroll in majors that lead to high paying jobs
    c. women probably suffer from their smaller stature
    d. b and c
    e. all of the above

17. The percentage of all births that occur out of wedlock is termed the:
    a. illegitimacy ratio
    b. legitimacy ratio
    c. fecundity ratio
    d. crude birth rate
    e. crude birth ratio

18. The shortage of black males results from:
   a. higher infant mortality
   b. more black females being born than black males
   c. the high mortality of young black men from accidents, drugs, and violence
   d. a and c
   e. all of the above

19. Which of the following is/are true about the black family?
   a. the black family was broken up by slavery
   b. sexual promiscuity was the norm on southern plantations
   c. the signs of severe disruption of the black family are very recent
   d. a and b
   e. none of the above

20. Conclusions drawn from this chapter include:
   a. all issues of gender are reciprocal
   b. gender inequalities are the same as inequalities between racial or ethnic groups
   c. gender inequalities occur between families, not within them
   d. b and c
   e. all of the above

Essays

1. A. Explain dyadic and structural power. (comprehension)
   B. Show how these may be used to explain the outcome of imbalanced sex ratios. (application)
   C. Integrate these concepts and show how they would explain changing sex roles today. (analysis)

2. A. Name three causes of imbalanced sex ratios. (knowledge)
   B. Using the example of either Athens or Sparta, show how these affected the role of women. (application)
   C. Contrast the role of women in ancient Athens and Sparta using Guttentag and Secord's theory. (analysis)

3. Trace the woman movement and the rise of feminism from its beginnings until today.

4. Explain three reasons for the gender gap as it occurs in the work force today.

5. Discuss how Guttentag and Secord's theory explains the position of the black family today.

Answers

Completion

1. sex ratio
2. low
3. low, high
4. female infanticide
5. less
6. males
7. differential life expectancy, sexual practices
8. women, men
9. dyadic power
10. structural power
11. stronger, less
12. structural
13. older
14. dyadic power
15. short
16. less
17. younger
18. illegitimacy ratio
19. higher
20. suffragette

Multiple Choice

1. a
2. e
3. b
4. a
5. b
6. d
7. a
8. b
9. e
10. c
11. b
12. d
13. c
14. d
15. c
16. d
17. a
18. d
19. c
20. a

Review and Special Project

Review

This section has focused on social inequality and social stratification. It has discussed various sociological theories of stratification, different stratification systems, and the consequences of social inequality.

Special Project

The various social classes (and even groups occupying the different strata within the classes) often exhibit marked differences in life-style. Although these differences are not nearly as great as those that separated the classes in agrarian societies, they nevertheless continue to exist. Research has shown that the classes differ not only in obvious ways such as income and educational level but also in more subtle areas such as speech patterns, mortality rates, types of entertainment, and even preferences for particular brands of beer.

You may wish to speculate about some aspects of life-style that might exhibit class differences. Choose one or two areas and devise specific hypotheses about the nature of these relationships. Search the literature for studies that test your hypotheses. (Bibliographies in sociology texts would be a good place to begin your literature search. You will also want to consult the *Sociological Abstracts* during your study.)

If possible, you may also wish to obtain your own data through observation, interviews, or more unobtrusive measures such as noting television commercials and magazine advertisements geared to a target population. Once you have supported your hypothesis, you might explain this relationship by using some of the theories you have studied.

CHAPTER THIRTEEN

The Family

Overview

The chapter opens with a discussion of dominant themes of the universality and decline of the family. It then offers definitions of the term *family* and differentiates between nuclear and extended families. It discusses the four functions of the family before turning its attention to a discussion of the traditional European family. The theme of modernization (a major emphasis in later chapters) is discussed with emphasis on the transformation of the family and the effects of modernization on kinship and divorce. One-parent families are then discussed, and Patterson's work on the relationship between parenting practices and childhood deviance is highlighted as the "over-the-shoulder" example. (Again, the importance of attachments is emphasized in this research.) The chapter itself closes with a discussion of research in the area of remarriage. A special topic on the older family concludes the chapter.

Capsule Summary

Families are small clusters of males and females, adults and children. **Membership is** typically **determined** by **common ancestry** and **sexual unions**. Although its form may differ, the family appears to be **universal**. **Family forms** include both the **nuclear** family and the **extended** family. **Families** typically perform the **functions** of **reproduction, sexual regulation, economic cooperation**, and **education**. The **incest taboo** exists in every culture, although its form also differs among cultures.

It has been assumed that the family is experiencing **decline**, although recent research by **Shorter** found the **traditional European family** to be almost the **exact opposite** of the **large, close, loving, extended** family it was long thought to be. Families were **smaller** than originally thought since **infant** and **childhood mortality was high, children left home early, and adults often died before becoming old**. **Privacy** was **nonexistent**; families lived in one room often shared with outsiders. **Attachments between parents** and **children** were **weak**, and neglect was common. Relationships between **spouses** were **indifferent** or **hostile**. Peer group bonds were strong and served as the primary emotional attachments. **Modernization** brought about major **changes**. **Romantic love** rather than economic ties became the basis for **marriage**; emotional bonds between **children** and **parents** also strengthened. The family of today is a result of these changes.

The **divorce rate** has risen markedly. Factors contributing to this rise include the **emphasis** on **romantic love** as the primary bond between spouses, the **entrance** of large numbers of **women** into the **work force**, and the **increased opportunity to obtain a divorce**. Since approximately **two-thirds of all divorces occur among couples** who have **children**, much attention has been focused on the **one-parent family**. **One-parent families** result not only from **divorce** but also from the **death of a spouse** and from the **increasing number of single women becoming mothers**. Most one-parent homes are headed by **women**, and problems with **money** and **time** often plague the single parent.

It often has been assumed that children from one-parent homes are more prone to delinquency, but research in this area has produced mixed results. **Patterson**, in his study of **deviant children**, found that the deviance is a result of **poor parenting** rather than family structure. **Parents** of **deviant children** often **lack close attachments** to them and often **deny** or **fail** to **punish their deviant acts**.

More than **80 percent** of Canadians and Americans who divorce remarry. Recently research has been conducted in the area of **conjugal careers**, and studies such as those by **Jacobs and Furstenberg** and **White and Booth** have focused on the **economic characteristics** of **second spouses** and the **effects of stepchildren in the home** on the **likelihood of divorce**.

Key Concepts

Be prepared to explain the concepts listed here. You should be able to provide several examples of each concept.

Key Research Studies

You should be familiar with both the methodology and the results of the following research studies. The data on the older family appears in Special Topic 4.

Completion

1. Sociological writing on the family has been dominated by the themes of _____ and _____.

2. The four primary functions of the family include sexual relationships, reproduction, _____ and _____.

3. A formal commitment to maintain a long-term relationship involving specific rights and responsibilities is termed _____.

4. An adult couple and their children are a(n) _____ family.

5. Virtually every society contains a(n) _____, which prohibits sexual relations between certain family members.

6. Family members such as the elderly and children who cannot support themselves are termed _____.

7. *The Making of the Modern Family* was written by _____.

8. The primary unit of sociability and attachment in the traditional European family was the _____.

9. The high divorce rate indicates that the marital relationship has become much _____ important than it used to be.

10. Approximately _____ of divorces occur among couples who have children.

11. Sociologists attribute the high divorce rates to the fact that romance is a highly perishable commodity and to _____.

12. Women who are age 30 and older when they give birth to their first child are termed _____.

13. The proportion of children born to unwed mothers is termed the _____.

14. More than 90 percent of one-parent families are headed by _____.

15. Research has found that _____ is a primary cause of deviant behavior among children.

16. A major problem faced by female-headed families is lack of _____.

17. A major problem experienced by parents with poor parenting skills is a lack of _____ of parents to their children.

18.* Americans over 65 are _____ likely than younger people to say they are very happy.

19.* People over 65 are almost _____ as likely as younger people to be pretty satisfied with their present financial situation.

20. If there are no stepchildren in the home, couples who remarry _____ have a higher rate of divorce than people who are marrying for the first time.

*Note: Questions 18 and 19 are drawn from Special Topic 4.

Multiple Choice

1. Murdock defined the family as a social group characterized by:
   a. common residence
   b. adults of both sexes
   c. reproduction
   d. a and c
   e. all of the above

2. Primary functions of the family include:
   a. economic cooperation among members
   b. sexual relationships
   c. reproduction
   d. b and c
   e. all of the above

3. An extended family is:
   a. larger than a nuclear family
   b. composed of more than one nuclear family
   c. composed of an adult couple and its children
   d. a and b
   e. none of the above

4. The theme of the decline of the family:
   a. has been supported by recent research by Shorter
   b. argues that the functions of the family are best met by the modern family
   c. is obvious when the contemporary family is compared with the traditional family
   d. a and c
   e. none of the above

5. Which of the following is/are true about sexual gratification as a function of the family?
   a. all societies have norms governing sexual behavior
   b. all societies have very narrow limits on who may engage in sex
   c. sexual norms often change very rapidly
   d. a and c
   e. all of the above

6. Which of the following is/are research findings of Shorter's study?
   a. the extended family living in a single household was typical regardless of economic level
   b. the traditional household was much smaller than had been assumed
   c. female-headed households were very rare when compared with today
   d. all of the above
   e. none of the above

7. Shorter found that the size of the traditional family was smaller than previously assumed because:
   a. infant and childhood mortality was high
   b. children often left home early
   c. adults often died before reaching "old age"
   d. a and c
   e. all of the above

8. Shorter found that relations between husbands and wives and parents and children:
   a. were based on emotional rather than economic ties
   b. were often characterized by indifference or even hostility
   c. were stronger than relationships to peer group members
   d. a and c
   e. none of the above

9. In the traditional European family strong emotional attachments were primarily between:
   a. persons of the same sex and outside the family
   b. mothers and young children
   c. husbands and wives
   d. elderly parents and adult children
   e. brothers and sisters

10. Effects of modernization on the family include:
   a. an increase in privacy for families
   b. a decrease in the importance of emotional ties as the basis for marriage
   c. an increase in the importance of peer group relations
   d. a and c
   e. none of the above

11. According to Table 13-3 (the quality of family relations based on the frequency of socializing by family members):
    a. few adult Americans frequently socialize with living parents
    b. almost two-thirds of married Americans rate their marriage as "very happy"
    c. as the family has grown smaller, family ties have severely weakened
    d. a and c
    e. none of the above

12. More than _____ of those who divorce remarry:
    a. 10 percent
    b. 50 percent
    c. 80 percent
    d. 90 percent
    e. 98 percent

13. Factors that have led to an increased divorce rate include:
    a. the increased opportunity to get divorced
    b. an increase in the importance of emotional ties as the basis for marriage
    c. the increased financial independence of women
    d. a and c
    e. all of the above

14. "Mature mothers":
    a. are women who are age 30 and over when they give birth to their first child
    b. are typically poorly educated
    c. are overwhelmingly career women
    d. a and c above
    e. all of the above

15. The recent influx of women into the labor force:
    a. contributes to a low birth rate
    b. has produced the phenomenon known as the "mature mother"
    c. reflects a low birth rate
    d. a and c
    e. all of the above

16. Patterson found that deviant children:
    a. had always been raised in a one-parent family
    b. were often greatly loved by their parents but that this attachment was not returned
    c. often had parents with poor parenting skills
    d. a and b
    e. none of the above

17. Patterson found that parents of problem children:
    a. have weak attachments to their children
    b. often fail to punish their children for failing to obey
    c. often refuse to "see" what their children are doing
    d. all of the above
    e. none of the above

18. According to Jacobs and Furstenberg:
    a. women overwhelmingly better their economic situation by remarriage
    b. on the average women marry second husbands who are no more and no less successful than their first husbands
    c. a woman with children under age 10 is in the best position to improve her economic situation by remarriage
    d. a and c
    e. a and b

19. According to research by White and Booth:
    a. stepchildren leave home at a younger age than do biological children
    b. couples who remarry have a higher divorce rate than people who are marrying for the first time if there are not stepchildren in the home
    c. couples who remarry do not have a higher rate of divorce than people who are marrying for the first time if there are not stepchildren in the home
    d. a and b
    e. a and c

20.* Research on the older family has shown:
    a. older Americans are the happiest Americans
    b. older Americans are overwhelmingly dissatisfied with their income
    c. older Americans are less likely to attend church weekly than younger Americans
    d. all of the above
    e. none of the above

*Note: Question 20 is drawn from Special Topic 4.

Essay

1. A. Name the four functions of the family. (knowledge)
   B. Discuss the theme of the universality of the family. (comprehension)
   C. Contrast the nuclear family with the extended family. (analysis)

2. A. Discuss some of the characteristics of the traditional European family as described by Shorter. (comprehension)
   B. Contrast the typical view of the extended family with the traditional family described by Shorter. (application)
   C. Relate the theme of decline to your discussion. (analysis)

3. Explain the following statement: "The current high divorce rate . . . could mean that at any given moment the great majority of marriages are happy ones."

4. Describe the changes in the family brought about by modernization.

5. Discuss five research findings about older Americans as these were described in Special Topic 4.

Answers

Completion
1. universality, decline
2. economic cooperation education (socialization)
3. marriage
4. nuclear
5. incest taboo
6. dependents
7. Edward Shorter
8. peer group
9. more
10. two-thirds
11. the increased opportunities to get divorced
12. mature mothers
13. illegitimacy ratio
14. a female or woman
15. poor parenting
16. income
17. attachments
18. more
19. twice
20. do not

Multiple Choice
1. e
2. e
3. d
4. e
5. d
6. b
7. e
8. b
9. a
10. a
11. b
12. c
13. e
14. d
15. e
16. c
17. d
18. b
19. e
20. a

CHAPTER FOURTEEN

Religion

Overview

This chapter opens with a discussion of the nature of religion and how it differs from other systems of explanation. It describes how religion makes norms legitimate and serves as a major force in creating moral communities. It introduces the concept of a religious economy and considers church-sect theory in depth. Chapter 14 discusses secularization and its effects on both sect revival and cult formation. It also discusses the American religious economy and cites numerous research findings by the author and others about sect and cult formation and concentration in both America and Europe. A brief discussion of the universal appeal of religion concludes the chapter. The importance of attachments is, again, a recurrent theme in this chapter, and considerable attention is payed to the relationship between attachments and religious application.

Capsule Summary

Religion consists of socially organized patterns of **beliefs** and **practices** concerning questions of **ultimate meaning** that assume the existence of the **supernatural**. Evidence that religion existed 100,000 years ago has been found in the remains of Neanderthal culture. **Religion** serves to make **norms legitimate** by explaining **why they exist** and **should be followed**.

As **societies** grew more **complex**, many different religions emerged, often side by side, thus creating **pluralistic religious economies**. **Weber** distinguished between the concepts of **church** and **sect**. Further elaborations of **church-sect theory** by Niebuhr and Johnson postulate that **churches** are characterized by **intellectualized teachings**, **emotional restraint** in services, and deities who are **remote** from **human affairs**. They exist in a state of relatively **low tension** with the sociocultural environment. **Sects**, on the other hand, embrace **emotionalism, fundamentalism,** and **personal relationships** with **deities**. They tend to exist in a state of **high tension** with the sociocultural environment.

Secularization involves turning away from **religion** to a **secular** view of life. Initially, many people thought that increased **secularization** would lead to the **eventual decline of religion**. Recent research has not supported this argument. Although secularization does lead to a decline in dominant religious organizations, such as **churches**, **sects** and **cults** often emerge to take their place. **Sects** differ from **cults** in that sects are **revivals** of an old religion. (The term **revival** is used to indicate sect formation.) **Cults**, on the other hand, are **new religions** and emerge as a result of **innovation**. **Charisma** is the ability of some people to inspire faith in others, and **charismatic leaders** are often very instrumental in **religious movements**.

The **North American religious economy** is **very diverse**. Church attendance is **high**, and almost two-thirds of all North Americans are members of a local congregation. **Sect**

formation is common since many of the dominant organizations are experiencing decline. **Sect movements** are clustered where **church membership** is **highest** because they represent a **revival** of an **already established religion**. Because **cults** represent a **new religion**, they experience greatest success in areas where **church attendance is low**, such as in the "unchurched belt" of the Pacific region. Cults often attract people who have no previous religious affiliation. Thus, rather than leading to a decline in religion itself, secularization has led to **sect** and **cult formation** as a response to the **decline** of the **dominant religious organizations**. **Similar** findings have been **reported in Europe**, thus further **strengthening this cyclical theory**.

Key Concepts

You should be able to explain the following concepts and be prepared to cite several examples of each concept.

Questions about ultimate meaning 406	Secularization 413
Religion 408	Revival 416
Supernatural 408	Innovation (cult formation) 416
Religious economy 410	Cult 416
Pluralism 410	Religious movement 416
Church 411	Charisma 417
Sect 411	Unchurched belt 420

Key Research Studies

You should be familiar with both the methodology and the results of the research studies cited here.

Stark, Bainbridge, and others: relationship between church membership and various forms of deviation; application of church-sect theory to the concept of a religious economy; studies of rates of church membership, religious affiliation, and cult formation 409, 420, 424

Nock: success of Canadian sect movements 428

Key Figures

Be able to associate each person with his contribution.

H. Richard Niebuhr: church-sect theory
Max Weber: concepts of church, sect, and charisma
Benton Johnson: modification of church-sect theory

Key Theories

Be able to explain the assumptions of these theories and, when applicable, cite related research findings.
    Church-sect theory
    Religious economy

Completion

1. The marketplace of competing faiths within a society is termed a _____.

2. All religions involve answers to questions about _____.

3. Religion entails socially organized patterns of beliefs and practices concerning ultimate meaning and assumes the existence of the _____.

4. The natural state of a _____ is religious pluralism.

5. _____ first distinguished between churches and sects.

6. _____ intellectualize religious teachings and restrain emotionalism in their services.

7. Sects stress _____ and individual mystic experience and tend toward _____.

8. Niebuhr argued that _____ provide for the religious needs of persons low in the stratification system.

9. Johnson suggested that church and sect are opposite poles on an axis representing the degree of tension between religious organizations and their _____.

10. Churches are religious bodies with relatively _____ tension, whereas sects are religious bodies with relatively _____ tension.

11. A turning away from religious to secular explanations of life is termed _____.

12. The process of the formation of sects is termed _____.

13. Revival is often a response to _____.

14. A religious movement that represents a new and unconventional faith is termed a(n) _____.

15. Weber termed the ability of some people to inspire faith in others _____.

16. Membership in conventional religious groups will be highest where _____ are most active.

17. In the United States and Canada, church membership is lowest in the _____.

18. As religious bodies deemphasize the _____, they seem less able to satisfy religious needs.

19. Studies have found that _____ abound in places where church attendance is lowest.

20. _____ do best when they tap into a strong religious tradition, whereas _____ abound where the conventional religious tradition is weak.

Multiple Choice

1. Most sociologists agree that religion always entails:
   a. answers to questions of ultimate meaning
   b. the existence of the supernatural
   c. the belief in one supreme deity
   d. a and b
   e. all of the above

2. Religious institutions:
   a. can be a major force in holding societies together
   b. can give legitimacy and reason to the norms
   c. can give divine sanctions to the other institutions
   d. a and b
   e. all of the above

3. The natural state of a religious economy is:
   a. pluralism
   b. oligarchy
   c. monopoly
   d. monarchy
   e. anarchy

4. Churches:
   a. intellectualize religious teachings
   b. stress emotionalism
   c. tend toward fundamentalism in their teachings
   d. b and c
   e. all of the above

5. Sects:
    a. represent the gods as close at hand
    b. stress individual mystical experiences
    c. restrain emotionalism in their services
    d. a and b
    e. all of the above

6. Niebuhr argued that sects provide for the religious needs of people:
    a. of low status
    b. in the middle class
    c. in the upper class
    d. with high educational levels
    e. b and c

7. Johnson argued that _____ are religious bodies with relatively high tension.
    a. cults
    b. sects
    c. churches
    d. a and b
    e. all of the above

8. Traditionally many social scientists believed that secularization would:
    a. lead to the eventual disappearance of religion
    b. increase membership in churches rather than sects
    c. foster the rise of cults
    d. increase membership in sects
    e. c and d

9. The formation of sects is termed:
    a. revelation
    b. revival
    c. secularization
    d. pluralism
    e. innovation

10. Responses to secularization include:
    a. revival
    b. cult
    c. religious change
    d. a and b
    e. all of the above

11. Sects are:
    a. new religions
    b. based on religions outside the conventional religious tradition
    c. new organizations reviving an old religion
    d. a and b
    e. none of the above

12. For *contemporary* sociologists of religion the basis of charisma is:
    a. the ability to inspire faith in others
    b. the ability to get others to believe one's message
    c. the unusual ability to form attachments with others
    d. a and b
    e. none of the above

13. Research has found that almost _____ of North Americans are official members of a local congregation.
    a. four-fifths
    b. three-quarters
    c. two-thirds
    d. one-half
    e. one-third

14. Sect movements are clustered in those states where:
    a. membership in Christian churches is low
    b. membership in Christian churches is high
    c. church attendance is low
    d. a and c
    e. none of the above

15. In the United States the "unchurched belt" is located in:
    a. the Deep South
    b. the Far West
    c. the Northeast
    d. the Middle West
    e. none of the above

16. In the United States, religious innovation is more common and successful in _____ than elsewhere in the nation.
    a. the Deep South
    b. the Far West
    c. the Northeast
    d. the Middle West
    e. New England

17. Which of the following statements is/are true?
    a. people who claim no religious affiliation are primarily nonbelievers
    b. people who say they have no religion are least likely to express faith in unconventional supernatural beliefs
    c. cults abound in areas where church attendance is highest
    d. all of the above
    e. none of the above

18. In contrast to the United States, the Canadian religious economy:
    a. is characterized by low church membership
    b. is more diverse than that of the United States
    c. is less diverse than that of the United States
    d. has experienced a decline in sect-like groups and a growth in denominations
    e. none of the above

19. Nock's Canadian data found:
    a. all Canadian sects do best where religious affiliation is highest
    b. conventional Protestant sects were strongest in provinces where the people were least likely to say they had no religion
    c. conventional Protestant sects were strongest in provinces where cult movements were doing best
    d. all Canadian sects do best in a more secularized environment
    e. none of the above

20. Today the average cult convert is likely to be:
    a. unusually well educated with excellent career potential
    b. poorly educated
    c. a social outcast
    d. b and c
    e. none of the above

Essay

1. A. Define religion. (knowledge)
    B. Discuss the nature of religion. (comprehension)
    C. Contrast religion with other systems of explanation. (analysis)

2. A. Define a religious economy. (knowledge)
    B. Explain the statement "The natural state of a religious economy is pluralism." (comprehension)
    C. Apply the concept of a religious economy to the United States and Canada. (application)

3. Explain Niebuhr's church-sect theory. Discuss the later modifications of this theory.

4. How does the process of secularization lead to sect and cult formation?

5. Distinguish between a sect and cult. Discuss two research findings about geographical concentrations of sects and cults.

Answers

Completion
1. religious economy
2. ultimate meaning
3. supernatural
4. religious economy
5. Max Weber
6. churches
7. emotionalism, fundamentalism
8. sects
9. sociocultural environment
10. low, high
11. secularization
12. revival
13. secularization
14. cult
15. charisma
16. sects
17. Far West (Pacific region)
18. supernatural
19. cults
20. sects, cults

Multiple Choice
1. d
2. e
3. a
4. a
5. d
6. a
7. b
8. a
9. b
10. e
11. c
12. c
13. c
14. b
15. b
16. b
17. e
18. e
19. b
20. a

Politics and the State

Overview

Chapter fifteen begins with a discussion of the medieval practice of the "freedom of the commons" and traces how population changes led to the "tragedy of the commons." It then discusses the concept of collective goods and describes the functions of the state. It traces the rise of the state and describes efforts in both England and the United States to "tame the state." It discusses elitist and pluralist states and focuses on Mill's concept of the power elite. The chapter then turns its attention to public opinion and focuses on the Gallup Poll. Research in the area of gender and other preference is then included as the "over-the-shoulder" examples. The chapter closes with a discussion of ideology and its role in political behavior.

Capsule Summary

States function to **preserve internal order, maintain external security**, and **provide** for **collective goods**. Although some people have argued in favor of **anarchy**, most feel that the state is a necessary aspect of complex society. Because states use **coercion**, "**taming the state**"—that is, **limiting its powers**—has been a dominant historical issue. The histories of England and the United States contain numerous examples of this process, which entails the establishment of both a **clear set of rules** defining the limits of power and a **structure** designed to ensure that the rules are observed.

States are of two essential types: **elitist** and **pluralist**. **Elitist** states, which are characterized by the **rule of a single elite** (sometimes termed the **power elite**), are the most common type. **Pluralist states**, on the other hand, are composed of many elites competing for power. In such states **power** is distributed among various **shifting coalitions**.

Public opinion polls, notably the **Gallup Poll**, are key indicators of **public opinion** about political issues. They are used extensively today to tap information about **voter preference**. Recent research has focused on the relationship between **gender** and **voter preference**. Although many have argued that female candidates may not be successful because of their gender, research by **Hunter** and **Denton** and by **Ekstrand** and **Eckert** have found that the relationship between **gender** and **vote getting** is **spurious**, and other factors are influential in this pattern.

Ideologies, theories about how societies should be run, do not enjoy the popular appeal in the United States and Canada that they do in Europe. Indeed, the results of **panel studies** have shown that Americans do not often maintain the same ideological conviction over time. Often **political interest** here takes the form of interest in a **specific issue** rather than an underlying **ideology**, and the term **issue public** has been used to identify groups actively involved in a particular issue. Indeed, rather than being strongly **ideological**, like their

European counterparts, **successful political parties** in America are really **coalitions of many internal issue publics**.

Key Concepts

You should be prepared to explain these concepts and be able to cite several examples of each concept.

"Freedom of the commons" 432
Public goods (collective goods) 436
State 437
Anarchy 439
Semistate 440
Pluralism 442
Tyranny of the minority 443
Tyranny of the majority 443

System of checks and balances 444
Elitist state 444
Pluralist state 444
Power elite 446
Representative government 448
Ideology 457
Panel study 460
Issue public 461

Key Research Studies

Be familiar with both the methodology and the results of the research studies cited here.

Messick and Wilke: laboratory re-creation of "freedom of the commons" 435
Gallup Poll data on political participation 450
Hunter and Denton: gender and vote getting ability 451
N.O.R.C. General Social Survey: gender and vote getting 454
Ekstrand and Eckert: gender and voting experiment 455
Wuthnow, Stark, and Bainbridge: ideology and attitudes 456

Key Figures

You should be able to associate each person with his contribution.

Mancur Olsen: relationship between public goods and coercion
Thomas Hobbes: *The Leviathan*
James Madison: tyranny of the minority, tyranny of the majority, system of checks and balances
Plato: concept of philosopher-king
C. Wright Mills: *The Power Elite*
George Gallup: opinion polls

Key Theories

Know how to explain the assumptions of these theories and, when applicable, cite related research findings.
    Pluralist theory
    Development of the state (not literally a theory)

Completion

1. Olsen argued that in order to create _____ or _____ goods the interests of the individual and the interests of the group collide.

2. The _____ or _____ is the organized embodiment of political processes within a society.

3. Only through organized _____ can humans assure themselves of public goods.

4. The practice in medieval England of allowing tenants to use all uncultivated pasture lands was termed _____.

5. Thomas Hobbes, in his book _____ describes what life would be like in a condition of anarchy.

6. In order for people to live in groups, internal order must be maintained, protection must be secured from external dangers, and _____ must be provided.

7. The existence of states rests on the development of _____.

8. _____ occurs when political power is dispersed among groups with diverse interests.

9. The danger that a majority of citizens will use the machinery of representative government to exploit and abuse minorities is termed _____.

10. The system known as _____ ensures that within the three branches of government each branch has the power to nullify actions taken by the other two.

11. The _____ state is the most common type.

12. In a _____ state rules governing state power are maintained by the existence of many competing elite.

13. Mills argued that the United States is ruled effectively by a small set of influential people who hold the preponderance of power termed the _____.

14. Research by Hunter and Denton has found that the relationship between gender and vote getting is _____.

15. In a _____ study the same sample of respondents is interviewed several times.

16. A connected set of strongly held beliefs based on a very few abstract ideas is termed a(n) _____.

17. Converse used the term _____ to identify those who take interest in and who participate at least as observers in discussions of an issue.

18. Successful parties are coalitions of many internal _____.

19. Compared with politics in Europe, politics in the United States _____ very ideological.

20. The first successful effort to conduct a public opinion poll that correctly predicted the outcome of a presidential election was led by _____.

Multiple Choice

1. In order for a group to survive:
    a. internal order must be maintained
    b. it must be secure from external dangers
    c. public goods must be provided
    d. a and b
    e. all of the above

2. Research by Messick and Wilke ("freedom of the commons" simulation) found:
    a. the subjects tended to use their power to exploit others
    b. the subjects behaved markedly different than had the English lords
    c. the leaders in the experiment gave themselves smaller shares than they gave others
    d. all of the above
    e. none of the above

3. Which of the following statements is/are true about the rise of the state?
    a. the existence of states rests on the development of agriculture
    b. agrarian states have a low degree of stratification
    c. in small, simple societies the state is often a loosely organized authority structure based on kinship and age
    d. a and c
    e. all of the above

4. As societies become more complex:
   a. the machinery of state becomes less elaborate but more specialized
   b. the machinery of state becomes less elaborate and less specialized
   c. the machinery of state becomes more elaborate and more specialized
   d. fewer people hold positions as full-time leaders
   e. none of the above

5. In a condition of _____ political power is dispersed among groups with diverse interests.
   a. monarchy
   b. pluralism
   c. anarchy
   d. authoritarian rule
   e. communalism

6. _____ theory of the state holds that private property is the root of all repression and exploitation by the ruling class.
   a. Marxist
   b. Pluralist
   c. Anarchist
   d. Functionalist
   e. Weberian

7. Madison termed the danger that a privileged few would use the machinery of representative government to exploit and abuse the many:
   a. tyranny of the majority
   b. tyranny of the minority
   c. anarchy
   d. pluralist tyranny
   e. none of the above

8. In a pluralist state:
   a. rules governing state power are maintained by the existence of many competing elites
   b. all persons living in the state have an equal amount of power in decision making
   c. shifting coalitions of many minorities rule
   d. a and c
   e. none of the above

9. According to Mills, the power elite in the United States is predominately:
   a. Protestant
   b. male
   c. educated in Ivy League schools
   d. a and c
   e. all of the above

10. The rise of opinion polling is most closely associated with:
    a. Thomas Hobbes
    b. George Gallup
    c. C. Wright Mills
    d. Thomas Jefferson
    e. David Reisman

11. According to research by Hunter and Denton (gender and vote getting):
    a. political parties start losing because they nominate women
    b. after political parties start losing they increase their rate of female nominations
    c. the effect of gender on vote getting may be spurious
    d. b and c
    e. all of the above

12. Research by Ekstrand and Eckert (experiment in gender and voting) has shown:
    a. the gender of the candidate did not seem to matter
    b. the gender of the student subject had a strong effect on that subject's preference
    c. the students strongly favored conservative candidates
    d. b and c
    e. all of the above

13. An ideology:
    a. is a connected set of strongly held beliefs based on a few abstract ideas
    b. is used to guide one's reaction to external events
    c. is essentially a theory about life
    d. all of the above
    e. b and c

14. A study in which the same sample of respondents is interviewed several times is termed a _____ study.
    a. retrospective
    b. case
    c. panel
    d. ex post facto
    e. none of the above

15. Converse used the term _____ to identify those who take an interest in and who participate at least as observers in discussions of an issue.
    a. interest groups
    b. ideology supporters
    c. interest publics
    d. issue publics
    e. support groups

16. Many people lack political ideologies because:
    a. people rarely invent their own
    b. ideologies are intellectual creations often involving many different authors and interpreters
    c. only elites can create and preserve ideologies
    d. all of the above
    e. none of the above

17. In the United States and Canada successful political parties:
    a. are strongly ideological
    b. appeal to a narrow interest group within an electorate
    c. are coalitions of many internal issue publics
    d. a and b
    e. none of the above

18. Research on gender and voter preference found:
    a. women are more likely to say they would vote for a female presidential candidate than men would
    b. women over 65 are more likely to say they would vote for a female presidential candidate than men over 65 would
    c. today over 75 percent of the subjects said they would vote for a qualified woman for president
    d. all of the above
    e. none of the above

19. Elitist states:
    a. are nonexistent today
    b. never call themselves democracies
    c. are the most common type
    d. b and c
    e. none of the above

20. Who of the following is not correctly paired with his contribution?
    a. Thomas Hobbes: *The Leviathan*
    b. James Madison: system of checks and balances
    c. George Gallup: the desirability of anarchy
    d. Plato: concept of philosopher-king
    e. none of the above

Essay

1. A. Name the two types of states. (knowledge)
   B. Give examples of elitist and pluralist states. (comprehension)
   C. Contrast elitist states with pluralist states. (analysis)

2. A. Name three functions of the state. (knowledge)
   B. Explain Olsen's argument about the necessity of coercion. (comprehension)
   C. Apply his argument to the "taming of the state." (application)

3. Trace the taming of the state in England and the United States.

4. What is a political ideology? Compare and contrast political and religious ideologies. Explain the statement "Compared with Europe, politics in the United States is not very ideological."

5. Explain the statement "Election day results do not mirror public opinion."

Answers

Completion

1. public, or collective
2. state, government
3. coercion
4. freedom of the commons
5. *Leviathan*
6. public (collective) goods
7. agriculture
8. pluralism
9. tyranny of the majority
10. checks and balances
11. elitist
12. pluralist
13. power elite
14. spurious
15. panel
16. ideology
17. issue publics
18. issues publics
19. is not
20. Gallup

Multiple Choice

1. e
2. a
3. d
4. c
5. b
6. a
7. b
8. d
9. e
10. b
11. d
12. a
13. d
14. c
15. d
16. d
17. c
18. c
19. c
20. c

CHAPTER SIXTEEN

The Interplay Between Education and Occupation

Overview

After opening with a discussion of the interplay between education and occupation, this chapter discusses the prestige rankings of occupations. It examines the changing nature of work and the composition of the labor force. Chapter 16 discusses unemployment and focuses on the relationship between the changing nature of work and rates of unemployment. It then considers the history of education in America and the current concern with the decline in the quality of education; the issue of the importance of schools and the related research of Coleman and Heyns are discussed. The chapter closes with an in-depth discussion of Meyer's theory of educational functions.

Capsule Summary

The **interplay** of **education** and **occupation** is a dominant feature of societies. **Education** has always **been highly** valued in America. Its importance has increased as we have moved from predominately **an industrial economy** to a **knowledge economy**. Typically those whose educational level is high enjoy not only greater income but also greater prestige; a person's **occupation** is a **major source of prestige**. Prestige rankings, which tend to be relatively consistent over time and place, have shown that the more training or skill required for an occupation, the higher its prestige.

During this century the **nature** of **work** and **education** has **changed**. More **positions** require **skill** and **extensive training**, and **fewer rely** on **physical labor**. Hence, **unemployment** rates for the **unskilled** are **high**. **Women** have entered the **work force** in **greater numbers**, partly as a response to the change in the nature of work. **More students** are staying in **school longer**; high school graduation is commonplace, and the majority of Americans enter college. With the increase in the number of people becoming better educated, there has been concern that the quality of education has diminished. Evidence from declining Scholastic Achievement Test (SAT) scores seems to support that claim.

Research has focused on the functions of schools. It has been long assumed that the quality of a school would have an effect on learning. **Coleman's** study, however, found that **school quality** had **no detectable impact** on **student achievement scores**.

Heyns found that **summer vacation** seemed to be **most detrimental** to **lower-income children**, who probably benefit the most from school. Further research by **Alexander et al.** and by Heyneman and Loxley have produced further evidence of the importance of **education** for the **disadvantaged**. There has been recent concern with the "**devaluation of education.**" **Collins** argues that the increasing emphasis on higher education may be creating a "**credential society.**" **Meyer's theory of educational functions** argues for the importance of education as a socializing agent. He concludes that the main function of education is to confer prestigious statuses and to train persons to play the roles attached to them.

Similarly, colleges have the power to create new positions that are accorded high prestige. For the occupants of these statuses, then, the prestige and life-style associated with them is not ended on graduation but rather becomes a lifelong identity.

Key Concepts

You should be ready to explain the concepts listed here, as well as be able to give several examples of each concept.

Occupational prestige 464

Scientific management 468

Unemployment 471

Education "deflation" 484

"Credential society" 485

Knowledge economy 487

Key Research Studies

You should be familiar with both the methodology and the results of the following research studies.

Hatt and North: occupational prestige rankings in the United States 464

Porter and Pineo: occupational prestige rankings in Canada 466

Taylor: time and motion studies 468

Coleman: quality of schools and student achievement scores 478

Heyns: the effects of summer vacation on learning 479

Alexander et al.: cognitive development of high school students and drop-outs 480

Heyneman and Loxley: school effect worldwide 481

N.O.R.C. General Social Survey: link between education and income 484

Key Theories

Know how to explain the assumptions of these theories and, when applicable, cite related research findings.

Allocation theories

Meyer's theory of educational functions

The following are not exactly theories per se, but knowledge of these trends and changes is essential for understanding this chapter.

The history of education in America

Changes in the composition of the work force

"Inflation" in higher education (Collins et al.)

Completion

1. Generally the more education people have, the _____ they earn and the _____ their occupational status.

2. The more training an occupation requires and the more pay it offers, the _____ its public prestige.

3. The application of scientific techniques to improve work efficiency is termed _____.

4. Technological innovations have made it possible to work _____.

5. According to Drucker, we are changing from a primarily industrial economy to a(n) _____ economy.

6. The term _____ is applied to those 16 years old and older who are without jobs and are seeking work.

7. Coleman found that school quality had little impact on student _____.

8. Collins argued that education was not meant to prepare people for careers but to protect _____.

9. Heyns found that schools greatly improve the situations of _____ children.

10. Heyns found that the single activity that is most strongly and consistently related to summer learning is _____.

11. Research by Alexander et al. found that dropping out of high school had the most severe negative effects on students from the most _____ backgrounds.

12. The _____ the nation, the greater the economic returns for getting an education.

13. As the level of education has risen in industrial nations, the relative advantage of completing a given level of education has _____.

14. Meyer argued that variations in school quality seem of _____ importance in the attitudes, values, opinions, and behaviors of graduates.

15. Meyer argued that the real impact of schools is to admit people to a particular _____.

16. _____ theories argue that education is a passive servant of the stratification system.

17. Meyer argued that education helps create new classes of _____ and _____, which then comes to be incorporated into society.

18. As more people get an education, a given level of education becomes _____ valuable.

19. The respect given a person on the basis of their job is termed _____.

20. Those persons who are employed or seeking employment make up the _____.

Multiple Choice

1. Studies of occupational prestige:
   a. yield results that are fairly stable over time and place
   b. have shown that many of the higher prestige positions require a college education
   c. have found that Canadians have a markedly different ranking system than Americans
   d. a and b
   e. b and c

2. The interplay between education and occupation:
   a. begins in adolescence
   b. begins early in life
   c. does not manifest itself until adulthood
   d. is declining as a result of "working smarter"
   e. none of the above

3. Drucker has argued:
   a. modern workers work harder and smarter than their grandparents
   b. we are changing from a primarily industrial economy to a knowledge economy
   c. we are changing from a knowledge economy to an industrial economy
   d. a and b
   e. none of the above

4. Reasons for the increased participation of women in the work force include:
   a. the feminist movement
   b. reduced fertility
   c. a change in the kinds of work available
   d. a and b
   e. all of the above

5. The labor force has expanded because:
   a. a greater proportion of young people are working today
   b. a greater proportion of older people are working today
   c. women have entered the work force
   d. a and c
   e. all of the above

6. The term *unemployed* includes only:
   a. those 16 and older
   b. those without jobs
   c. those who are seeking work
   d. a and b
   e. all of the above

7. Reasons for the high rates of unemployment among blacks include:
   a. discrimination
   b. the fact that blacks today are far less likely to enter college than whites
   c. the dwindling supply of unskilled labor jobs
   d. a and c
   e. all of the above

8. Coleman's study found that:
   a. school quality had a major impact on student achievement scores
   b. teachers' educational levels have a major impact on student achievement scores
   c. school quality did not have a major impact on student achievement scores
   d. summer vacation had little effect on students' achievement
   e. a and b

9. Today approximately _____ of Americans are in the labor force:
   a. 64 percent
   b. 75 percent
   c. 40 percent
   d. 88 percent
   e. 51 percent

10. A major reason for the decline in the intellectual quality of teachers is that:
    a. more women are becoming teachers
    b. minorities are increasingly entering the teaching profession
    c. changing sex roles are allowing highly talented women to enter professions other than teaching
    d. the proportion of teachers who are male is increasing
    e. none of the above

11. Heyns found that schools:
    a. merely maintain the differences that poor and middle-class children bring to schools
    b. greatly improve the situations of poor children
    c. greatly improve the situations of middle-class children but have little effect on poor children
    d. have little effect on either poor or middle-class children
    e. none of the above

12. Heyns's study of the effect of summer vacation found that:
    a. attending summer school prevents summer learning losses
    b. children from all levels were harmed by summer vacations
    c. children from higher-income families learned about as much during vacation as they did during the school year
    d. a and b
    e. none of the above

13. Research by Heyneman and Loxley in school effects in twenty-nine nations found:
    a. the poorer the nation, the less that students' backgrounds influence their school performances
    b. kids in less industrialized nations learn more during the same number of school years than those in more industrialized nations
    c. the poorer the nation the less the economic returns for getting an education
    d. a and b
    e. all of the above

14. The decline of the value of a college education can be attributed to:
    a. the result of colleges not preparing people for careers
    b. the rising relative earnings of blue-collar workers, which have surpassed the earnings of some college graduates
    c. the fact that college graduates are no longer a scarce commodity
    d. b and c
    e. all of the above

15. Meyer argued that:
    a. a major effect of education is that people learn to play the role appropriate to the status that their school confers on them
    b. the most powerful socializing property of schools is the ability to confer statuses that are recognized in the society at large
    c. educational institutions have the power to create new occupations and to control the placement of these occupations in the occupational structure
    d. all of the above
    e. none of the above

16. Allocation theorists argue that the primary purpose of education is to:
    a. place people in a particular status
    b. educate children
    c. serve as a passive servant of the stratification system
    d. a and c
    e. none of the above

17. _____ made an early attempt to apply scientific techniques to increase efficiency (scientific management):
    a. Frederick W. Taylor
    b. James Coleman
    c. Barbara Heyns
    d. Cecil North and Paul Hatt
    e. Ivan Illich

18. Collins has argued that:
    a. the expansion of higher education has created a "credential society"
    b. colleges impart training vital for the performance of many of the jobs that now demand a college degree
    c. credentials serve as a way to control entry to many positions
    d. a and c
    e. all of the above

19. Today women make up slightly over _____ of the labor force in the United States and Canada.
    a. 25 percent
    b 40 percent
    c. 55 percent
    d. 68 percent
    e. 75 percent

20. Long-term unemployment tends to be concentrated in:
    a. the Appalachia region of the United States
    b. the Pacific region of the United States and Canada
    c. minorities
    d. a and c
    e. all of the above

Essay

1. A. Name two functions of schools. (knowledge)
   B. Discuss Meyer's theory of educational functions. (comprehension)
   C. Contrast Meyer's theory with allocation theories. (analysis)

2. A. Explain the concept of a knowledge economy. (comprehension)
    B. Show the interplay of education and occupation in a knowledge economy. (application)
    C. Contrast an industrial economy with a knowledge economy. (analysis)

3. Trace the history of the educational system in America.

4. Discuss some of the findings of either Coleman's study or Heyns's study.

5. Discuss why the quality of education seems to have declined in recent years.

Answers

Completion
1. more, higher
2. greater
3. scientific management
4. smarter
5. knowledge
6. unemployed
7. achievement
8. class interests
9. poor
10. reading
11. disadvantaged
12. poorer
13. declined
14. little or no
15. educational status
16. allocation
17. knowledge, personnel
18. less
19. occupational prestige
20. labor force

Multiple Choice
1. d
2. b
3. b
4. e
5. c
6. e
7. d
8. c
9. a
10. c
11. b
12. c
13. a
14. d
15. e
16. d
17. a
18. d
19. b
20. d

Review and Special Project

Review

This section focused on the major social institutions: the family, religion, the political order, the economy, and education. It discussed not only the nature of these institutions but also emphasized changes in them.

Special Project

You might wish to investigate a specific change that you believe has occurred in one of these institutions during the past few decades. Possible topics for investigation might include the following:

1. The increase in the number of one-parent homes.
2. The change in the divorce rate of a particular category of persons (families with young children, people over age 50, and so on).
3. The increase (or decrease) in church attendance or membership in a specific denomination or sect.
4. The increase (or decrease) in political participation (voting rates, registration rates) of a particular group (persons under 30, blacks, and so on).
5. The increase (or decrease) in the number of women in a particular profession.

To ascertain these changes you will need to obtain data from 1940 or 1950 and then compare these statistics with more recent ones. Sociologists often make use of the wealth of information available from Gallup Polls, census data, and government reports when studying trends and changes over time. Most of these statistics are readily available through your school or public library. (You may be surprised to see the wide variety of information that is available.) You will also want to investigate research journals for specific studies in your area of investigation. The *Sociological Abstracts*, an index of articles published in major journals, is of great assistance in locating relevant articles.

Once you have obtained your data, you may want to investigate these trends further. You may wish to locate studies and theories that attempt to explain these changes within the context of general societal change.

CHAPTER SEVENTEEN

Social Change and Modernization

Overview

A discussion of modernization and sources of social change opens this chapter. It explains cultural lag and highlights the Iranian revolution as an example of this concept. It also describes capitalism as an economic system and contrasts capitalism with command economies. Chapter 17 then offers an in-depth discussion of four theories of modernization: the Marxist view, Weber on Protestantism and the emergence of capitalism, the state theory of modernization, and the world system (dependency) theory. Delacroix's test of dependency theory is included as the "over-the-shoulder" example. The chapter concludes with a special topic on stirrups and feudal domination.

Capsule Summary

Modernization is the process by which **agrarian societies** are transformed into **industrial societies**. Social systems undergo **change** from both **internal** and **external** sources. Internal sources of change include **innovations, new technology, new culture, new social structures, group conflict,** and **growth.** External sources include **diffusion, conflict,** and **ecological change. Cultural lag** often occurs during times of social change.

Despite their differences, all **theories** of **modernization** attribute modernization in the West to **capitalism.** In contrast to **command economies, capitalism** is characterized by **private ownership, competition** for **profits,** and a **free market.** Capitalism encourages an individual to produce as much as possible because it rewards hard work and reinvestment of profits.

Karl Marx attributed the **Industrial Revolution** to **capitalism.** He believed that **capitalism encouraged people** to **work harder** and **develop ideas,** thus **fostering technological advances.** Although he argued that **capitalism** was **necessary** for **modernization,** he believed that by promoting **self-interest,** capitalism fostered **alienation, inequality,** and **class conflict.** Marx believed that once modernization was accomplished, communist revolutions would foster collective ownership and allow the benefits of modernization to be shared equally.

Max Weber explained the emergence of **capitalism** as a result of religious doctrines of the **Protestant Reformation.** He argued that belief in **predestination** fostered an ideology that encouraged **production, thrift,** and the **reinvestment of profit.** Over time these values lost much of their religious significance and became basic secular values that were congruent with the economic system of capitalism.

The **state theory of modernization** argues that both **capitalism** and **Protestantism** are the result of the **taming of the state.** Repressive societes are characterized by command economies. As the power of the state is limited, people become freer to pursue economic self-interest; this in turn will encourage technological progress and capitalism. This theory argues that capitalism can emerge only once the state is tame.

In contrast to the preceding theories, **world system (dependency) theory** looks to **external** sources of change. It argues that in the world system stratification exists among nations. The **dominant** nations, termed **core nations**, exploit the weaker **peripheral** nations.

Core nations are highly modernized, and modernization in peripheral nations is hampered by this domination. In his test of the **dependency theory, Delacroix** did not find support for the assumptions of dependency theory.

Key Concepts

You should be able to explain the concepts listed here; you should also be able to give several examples of each concept.

Modernization 492	Empire 507
Innovation 494	Core nations 508
Cultural lag 497	Peripheral nations 508
Social evolution 499	Semi-peripheral nations 508
Diffusion 499	Dependency theory 508
Capitalism 503	Feudalism 519
Command economies 503	

Key Research Studies

Be familiar with both the methodology and the results of the following studies.
Delacroix: test of the dependency theory 510
Bradshaw: dependency effects 513

Key Figures

You should be able to associate each person with his contribution.
William F. Ogburn: concept of cultural lag
Max Weber: *The Protestant Ethic and the Spirit of Capitalism*
Martin Luther: Protestant Reformation
John Calvin: doctrine of predestination

Key Theories

Be prepared to explain the assumptions of these theories of modernization and, when applicable, cite related research findings.
   Karl Marx: capitalism
   Max Weber: the Protestant Ethic and the emergence of capitalism
   State theory of modernization
   World system (dependency) theory

Completion

1. The process by which agrarian societies are transformed into industrial societies is termed _____.

2. Diffusion is the transfer of _____.

3. Types of innovation that may cause social change include new technology, new culture, and new _____.

4. The delay between the change in one part of society that produces a realignment of the other parts may cause _____.

5. The concept of cultural lag is associated with _____.

6. External sources of change include diffusion, conflict, and _____.

7. An economic system based on private ownership of the means of production that relies on a free market is termed _____.

8. A unique feature of capitalism is that it relies on a _____.

9. Economies in which some people decide what work is to be done and order others to do it are termed _____.

10. The secret of capitalism is to reward _____.

11. _____ argued that the religious ideas produced by Protestantism motivated people to limit their consumption and pursue maximum wealth.

12. The state theory of modernization argues that _____ will always develop when the state is tame.

13. Chirot argued that the untamed state is incapable of not stifling economic development because it is incapable of not _____.

14. The doctrine of predestination is associated with _____.

15. _____ considers relationships among nations as a causative force in change.

16. Wallerstein argued that within the world system _____ exists among nations.

17. _____ nations have highly specialized economies, weak internal political structures, and a low standard of living for workers.

18. Wallerstein termed the dominant nations in the world system _____ nations.

19. Delacroix argued that modernization is influenced primarily by _____ processes.

20. The first effect of modernization on the less developed nations has been an immense _____ in recent decades.

Multiple Choice

1. Internal sources of social change include:
   a. innovations
   b. group conflicts
   c. growth
   d. a and c
   e. all of the above

2. New technology:
   a. may appear and go unused for a long time
   b. changes societies by itself
   c. can be a major source of social change
   d. a and c
   e. all of the above

3. Innovation may result in:
   a. new technology
   b. new culture
   c. new social structures
   d. a and c
   e. all of the above

4. The periods of delay between the time one part of society changes and the other parts realign is termed:
   a. diffusion delay
   b. cultural lag
   c. innovation lag
   d. cultural discontinuation
   e. none of the above

5. The term *cultural lag* is associated with:
   a. Max Weber
   b. Karl Marx
   c. William Ogburn
   d. John Calvin
   e. Immanuel Wallerstein

6. The transfer of innovations is termed:
   a. cultural lag
   b. diffusion
   c. accommodation
   d. social evolution
   e. assimilation

7. External sources of social change include:
   a. diffusion
   b. conflict
   c. changes in the physical environment
   d. a and b
   e. all of the above

8. An economic system based on private ownership of the means of production and a system by which people compete to gain profits is termed:
   a. capitalism
   b. communism
   c. socialism
   d. privateering
   e. command economy

9. Capitalism is *unique* in its:
   a. economic system based on private ownership of the means of production
   b. emphasis on competition to gain profits
   c. reliance on a free market
   d. emphasis on communal goods
   e. a and b

10. Command economies:
    a. rely on free market principles
    b. reward surplus production
    c. encourage consumption
    d. a and b
    e. all of the above

11. Capitalistic economies:
    a. rely on a free market
    b. encourage immediate consumption
    c. reward surplus production
    d. a and c
    e. all of the above

12. The doctrine of predestination is associated with:
    a. Martin Luther
    b. Karl Marx
    c. John Calvin
    d. Immanuel Wallerstein
    e. none of the above

13. Weber argued that:
    a. from its roots in the Protestant Ethic, capitalism blossomed
    b. capitalism became a secular ideology in its own right
    c. the Protestant Ethic was the sole cause of capitalism
    d. a and b
    e. all of the above

14. The state theory of modernization argues that:
    a. capitalism will develop when the state is tame
    b. Protestant theology led to the development of capitalism
    c. modernization is the result of changes introduced from other societies
    d. a and c
    e. all of the above

15. Theories that seek the causes of the Industrial Revolution *within* societies include:
    a. world system theory
    b. Marxist theory
    c. dependency theory
    d. b and c
    e. a and c

16. According to world system theory, core nations:
    a. have weak or unstable governments
    b. have a low standard of living for workers
    c. have highly diversified economies
    d. all of the above
    e. b and c

17. In his test of the dependency hypothesis, Delacroix found that:
    a. nations specializing in raw material exports showed as much an increase in per capita GNP as nations specializing in the export of manufactured goods
    b. modernization is influenced by external processes of the world system
    c. extensive support exists for the dependency hypothesis
    d. all of the above
    e. none of the above

18. According to world system theory:
    a. stratification exists among nations
    b. the class position of a nation is determined by its place in a geographical division of labor
    c. less developed nations are economically dominated by more developed ones
    d. all of the above
    e. none of the above

19. Which of the following is *not* correctly paired with his theory or contribution?
    a. William Ogburn—cultural lag
    b. Immanuel Wallerstein—state theory of modernization
    c. John Calvin—predestination
    d. Martin Luther—Protestant Reformation
    e. a and b

20.* In feudal societies, land ownership is based on _____ obligations.
    a. economic
    b. kinship
    c. military
    d. religious
    e. none of the above

*Note: Question 20 is drawn from Special Topic 5.

Essay

1. A. Name the four theories of modernization. (knowledge)
    B. Explain two of these theories. (comprehension)
    C. Compare and contrast two of these theories. (analysis)

2. A. Define cultural lag. (knowledge)
   B. Give several examples of cultural lag. (comprehension)
   C. Apply this concept to the Iranian Revolution. (application)

3. Discuss some internal and external sources of social change; give an example of each.

4. Explain Weber's theory of the relationship between the Protestant Ethic and the emergence of capitalism.

5. Explain world systems theory and show how Delacroix's study did not support the dependency hypothesis.

Answers

Completion
1. modernization
2. innovations
3. social structures
4. cultural lag
5. William Ogburn
6. ecological sources
7. capitalism
8. free market
9. command economies
10. surplus production
11. Weber
12. capitalism
13. overtaxing
14. Calvin
15. world system theory
16. stratification
17. peripheral
18. core
19. internal
20. population explosion

Multiple Choice
1. e
2. d
3. e
4. b
5. c
6. b
7. e
8. a
9. c
10. c
11. d
12. c
13. d
14. a
15. b
16. c
17. a
18. d
19. b
20. c

CHAPTER EIGHTEEN

Population Changes

Overview

This chapter begins by discussing demography and early uses of government census. It then focuses on the various rates and measures used by contemporary demographers. After examining preindustrial population trends and Malthusian theory, it discusses population changes resulting from modernization and focuses on the theory of demographic transition. Chapter 18 looks at the second population explosion and recent research by Berelson and by Cutright and Smith on the fertility decline in developing nations. It closes with a special topic section devoted to changes in society caused by the "baby boom."

Capsule Summary

Demography is the **study of population. Demographers** study not only **population size** but also population **changes** and **trends.** Although demographic theory has its roots in the work of **Adam Smith,** ancient governments often conducted a **census** (such as the **Domesday Book**) for tax purposes. Demographers today often use extensive measures such as **crude rates, specific rates, cohorts,** and **age** and **sex structures** to measure population trends and provide a basis for long-term planning.

Early societies often had a difficult time maintaining their populations. The **first** major **increase in population** occurred with the **development** of **agriculture.** Agricultural societies can produce more food and hence support greater numbers, but they are vulnerable to famines and disease, which serve to reduce their numbers. With the advent of **modernization,** a population explosion occurred as a result of both **agricultural innovations** and a marked decrease in the **mortality** rate.

Malthusian theory attempts to explain the periodic **growth** and **decline** of **populations** prior to **modernization.** It postulates that populations always grow to a size slightly above the available food supply. **Positive checks** such as disease and famine then reduce the population to a size congruent with the available food, and the cycle begins again.

The **theory** of **demographic transition** attempts to explain the population growth associated with modernization. This transition involves a change from the long-established pattern of high fertility and high but variable mortality to one of low fertility and low mortality. It argues that although modernization cuts the death rate, markedly, it also encourages decreased fertility as large families become a liability rather than an asset. **Cultural lag** may occur between the **initial decline** in the **mortality rate** and the **corresponding decline** in the **birth rate,** causing a temporary rapid increase in population. This has occurred in the past few decades in less developed countries, although recent research by **Berelson** and others had detected the beginning of a decline in fertility in some of these nations.

Key Concepts

You should be able to explain the following concepts, as well as be able to cite several examples of each concept.

Domesday Book 520
Census 522
Demography 522
Growth rate 523
Crude death rate 523
Crude birth rate 523
General fertility rate 523
Age-specific death rate 524
Birth cohort 525

Age structure 527
Sex structure 527
Expansive population structure 527
Stationary population structure 527
Constrictive structure 527
Positive checks 532
Replacement-level fertility 536
Zero population growth 536

Key Research Study

You should be familiar with both the methodology and the results of the research studies cited here.

Berelson: "thresholds" of modernization—fertility reduction among less developed nations 543

Cutright and Smith: population patterns of less developed nations 544

Key Figures

Be able to associate each person with his contribution.

William the Conqueror: *Domesday Book*
Adam Smith: foundations of demographic theory
Thomas R. Malthus: *Essay on the Principles of Population*
Kingsley Davis: theory of demographic transition
Paul Ehrlich: *The Population Bomb*

Key Theories

You should be able to explain the assumptions of these theories and, when applicable, cite related research findings.

Malthusian theory
Theory of demographic transition

Completion

1. A population count is termed a _____.

2. Demography is the study of _____.

3. The net population gain (or loss) divided by the size of population constitutes the _____.

4. The _____ can be computed by dividing the total number of deaths for a year by the total population for that year.

5. The total number of births divided by the total number of females within a certain age span is termed the _____.

6. All persons born within a given time period such as a year constitute the _____.

7. An expansive population structure is characteristic of present populations in _____ nations.

8. A declining population reflects a _____ population structure.

9. The first great shift in population trends was caused by the development of _____.

10. Sudden rises in mortality rates in primitive societies can be the result of war, _____, and _____.

11. *An Essay on the Principles of Population* was written by _____.

12. Malthus termed famine, disease, and war _____.

13. The second great shift in population was caused by the _____.

14. _____ fertility occurs when the number of births each year equals the number of deaths.

15. The theory of demographic transition is closely associated with _____.

16. As a result of modernization, children ceased to be a(n) _____ and became a(n) _____.

17. The fourth great shift in population trends was massive, unprecedented population growth in _____.

18. Cutright and Smith argued that until a life expectancy of 46 years is reached, there is no correlation between life expectancy and _____.

19. The proportions of males and females in a population is termed the _____.

20. The medieval census conducted by William the Conquerer following his takeover of England was termed the _____ *Book*.

Multiple Choice

1. The study of population is termed:
    a. ecology
    b. ethnology
    c. democracy
    d. demography
    e. none of the above

2. A population can decline because:
    a. births are increasing
    b. deaths are increasing
    c. people are migrating into a region
    d. all of the above
    e. a and c

3. The number of deaths in a year divided by the total population for that year is termed the:
    a. crude death rate
    b. general mortality rate
    c. age-specific death rate
    d. growth rate
    e. death cohort

4. All of the persons born in a given time period constitute the:
    a. crude birth rate
    b. age-specific birth rate
    c. general fertility rate
    d. growth rate
    e. birth cohort

5. An expansive population structure:
    a. reflects a declining population
    b. has fewer people on the bottom than in the middle
    c. is characteristic of underdeveloped nations
    d. a and b
    e. all of the above

6. A rapid increase in the death rate may be the result of:
   a. famine
   b. disease
   c. war
   d. all of the above
   e. none of the above

7. Which of the following have a positive effect on fertility?
   a. affluence
   b. religion
   c. the proportion of males in the population
   d. a and b
   e. all of the above

8. The first great shift in population trends was caused by:
   a. the modernization of agriculture
   b. the development of agriculture
   c. the decline in mortality due to better sanitation standards
   d. the introduction of technology
   e. none of the above

9. According to Malthus:
   a. population growth will tend to rise slightly above the supply of food
   b. fertility could be controlled through moral restraint
   c. both fertility and mortality periodically rise and fall
   d. a and c
   e. all of the above

10. According to Malthus, positive checks included:
    a. disease
    b. moral restraint
    c. war
    d. a and c
    e. all of the above

11. During the initial period of modernization:
    a. the industrialization of agriculture increased the food supply
    b. the population grew rapidly
    c. the mortality rate dropped markedly
    d. all of the above
    e. none of the above

12. Replacement level fertility:
    a. occurs when the number of births each year equals the number of deaths
    b. produces zero population growth as soon as the age structure has adjusted
    c. has yet to be reached in industrialized nations
    d. a and b
    e. all of the above

13. The demographic transition involves:
    a. a change from high fertility to low fertility
    b. a change from low fertility to high fertility
    c. a change from low mortality to high mortality
    d. b and c
    e. none of the above

14. Davis argued that modernization encourages low fertility because:
    a. the decline in infant and childhood mortality eliminated the need for families to have large numbers of children to ensure that some survived to adulthood
    b. large families became an asset rather than a burden
    c. birth control devices were invented early in the Industrial Revolution
    d. a and b
    e. all of the above

15. "Thresholds of modernization" include the characteristic(s) that:
    a. more than half of the labor force is not employed in agriculture
    b. 80 percent of the females age 15 to 19 are not married
    c. at least one-half of the adults can read
    d. a and b
    e. all of the above

16. The second population explosion:
    a. occurred in Western nations
    b. occurred during the 1970s and early 1980s
    c. resulted from a rapid drop in the mortality rate
    d. all of the above
    e. a and b

17. By the early 1970s, demographers detected a _____ in the less developed nations.
    a. fertility increase
    b. fertility decline
    c. mortality increase
    d. mortalitiy decline
    e. none of the above

18. The proportion of males and females in a population constitutes the:
    a. sex rate
    b. sex structure
    c. sex ratio
    d. fertility rate
    e. fertility ratio

19. An age structure in which younger cohorts are smaller than the ones before them is termed a(n) _____.
    a. stationary population structure
    b. constrictive population
    c. expansive population
    d. modernized population
    e. none of the above

20. Who of the following is not correctly paired with his contribution?
    a. Ehrlich: the *Domesday Book*
    b. Malthus: *Essay on the Principles of Population*
    c. Davis: theory of demographic transition
    d. all of the above
    e. none of the above

Essay

1. A. Define demography. (knowledge)
    B. Explain Malthusian theory. (comprehension)
    C. Contrast Malthusian theory with the theory of demographic transition. (analysis)

2. A. Define the theory of demographic transition. (knowledge)
    B. Using the concept of cultural lag, explain the second developing nations. (comprehension)
    C. Apply either the theory of demographic transition or Malthusian theory to the current situation in developing nations. (application)

3. Describe some of the population characteristics of preindustrial societies.

4. Discuss some of the changes that occurred during the first population explosion.

5.* Discuss some of the changes that have occurred as a result of the "baby boom."

*Note: This question is drawn from Special Topic 6.

Answers

Completion

1. census
2. population
3. growth rate
4. crude death rate
5. fertility rate
6. birth cohort
7. underdeveloped
8. constrictive
9. agriculture
10. disease, famine
11. Malthus
12. positive checks
13. Industrial Revolution
    (or modernization of agriculture)
14. replacement level fertility
15. Kinsley Davis
16. economic asset, economic burden
17. less developed nations
18. fertility
19. sex structure
20. *Domesday*

Multiple Choice

1. d
2. b
3. a
4. e
5. c
6. d
7. b
8. b
9. a
10. d
11. d
12. e
13. a
14. a
15. e
16. c
17. b
18. b
19. b
20. a

CHAPTER NINETEEN

Urbanization

Overview

After opening with a description of preindustrial cities, this chapter describes the impact of the agricultural revolution and industrialization on urban growth. It introduces the concept of a metropolis and distinguishes between the fixed-rail metropolis and the freeway metropolis. Ethnic neighborhoods are then discussed, highlighting both Park and Burgess's early theory and recent tests of that theory. The chapter then examines the work of early theorists such as Tönnies, Durkheim, and Wirth and cites relevant research. Chapter 19 ends with a discussion of both the macro effects and the micro effects of crowding.

Capsule Summary

Urbanization, the migration from rural areas to cities, was the result of **modernization**. Prior to the **agricultural revolution** and **industrialization**, cities were **small, dirty, disease-ridden**, and **crowded**. Despite these conditions people did migrate to preindustrial cities in search of **economic gain, adventure**, and **anonymity**. The **agricultural revolution** made it possible for larger numbers of people to live in the city; **specialization** also required a large urban work force.

Today the term **city** is rather nebulous. Because many people live in **suburbs** surrounding a city, the term **metropolis** (or **metropolitan area**) has come to refer to a **city** and its **sphere of influence**.

Modern cities have been shaped by **transportation**. Older industrial cities are termed **fixed-rail** metropolises since their growth followed the railroad lines outward from the center of the city. More recently, the **decentralized freeway** metropolis has emerged, and research indicates that people seem to prefer to reside in such an area.

Many cities contain ethnic and racial neighborhoods. The ethnic populations of these areas change over time due to a process termed **succession**. **Park** and **Burgess** argued that slum neighborhoods are occupied successively by the lowest status groups. **Guest** and **Weed**, using the **index of dissimilarity**, recently found support for this theory and concluded that the barriers to integration were economic rather than ethnic or racial. **Taeuber** recently reported that American cities have become less segregated as blacks have moved into the suburbs and white neighborhoods.

Early theorists took a negative view of the city. **Tönnies's** contrast of **Gemeinschaft** and **Gesellschaft** portrayed **Gesellschaft** relationships as cold and impersonal. **Durkheim** (and later **Wirth**) argued that urban areas were characterized by high rates of **anomie** and resulting deviance. However, recent research has failed to support the assumption that anomie is characteristic of urbanites.

Researchers have studied both **macro** effects and **micro** effects of crowding. Studies have not found any significant differences in pathology rates between areas of high and low population density. On the other hand, research by **Gove** and others found considerable support for **micro** effects of crowding.

Key Concepts

You should be able to explain the following concepts. You should also be able to cite several examples of each concept.

Urbanization 554	Fixed-rail metropolis 568
Preindustrial cities (characteristics) 554	Freeway metropolis 568
Specialization 564	Succession 572
Suburb 566	Index of dissimilarity 573
Metropolitan area (metropolis) 567	*Gemeinschaft* 576
Sphere of influence 567	*Gesellschaft* 576
Standard Metropolitan 567	Anomie 578
Statistical Area 567	

Key Research Studies

Be familiar with both the methodology and the results of the research studies cited here.

Darroch and Marston: test of theory of ethnic succession 572
Guest and Weed: economics and integration 573
Taeuber: test of Guest and Weed study 574
Faris and Dunham: neighborhood affluence and rates of mental illness 578
Macro studies of crowding 581
Gove and others: micro study of crowding 581

Key Theories

You should be able to explain the assumptions of these theories and, when applicable, cite related research findings.

Park, McKenzie, and Burgess: theory of ethnic succession
Tönnies: *Gemeinschaft* and *Gesellschaft*
Durkheim and Wirth: anomie theories

Completion

1. The migration of people from the countryside to the city is termed _____.

2. Urbanization is the result of the more general process of _____.

3. The successive occupation of slum neighborhoods by the lowest status groups is termed _____.

4. Limits of the size of preindustrial cities included poor transportation and _____.

5. _____ and urbanization are inseparable processes.

6. An elaborate division of labor to simplify production is termed _____.

7. If an area has a population of more than 2,500 demographers, classify it as a(n) _____.

8. The United States census classifies a community as a city when it has at least _____ residents.

9. A city and its suburbs with their central city as a single unit is termed a(n) _____.

10. The _____ of a city is the area whose inhabitants depend on the central city for jobs, recreations, and a sense of community.

11. The focal point of the _____ cities was the center of the city.

12. Decentralized cities, common in the western United States are termed _____.

13. The theory of ethnic succession was proposed by _____ and _____.

14. Park and Burgess proposed that ethnic and racial segregation in cities was based primarily on _____ and _____ differences.

15. Guest and Weed argued that _____ between groups seemed to be the primary neighborhood barrier.

16. _____ and _____ argued that urban areas are characterized by high rates of anomie.

17. Gove and others found support for _____ rather than theories of _____ crowding.

18. Tönnies used the term _____ to describe small cohesive communities.

19. Tönnies used the term *Gesellschaft* to describe the quality of life in _____ societies.

20. An urban place in the immediate vicinity of a city is termed a _____.

Multiple Choice

1. The size of preindustrial cities was limited by:
   a. disease
   b. poor transportation
   c. reliance on nearby farms to provide food
   d. a and b
   e. all of the above

2. Today approximately _____ of Americans and Canadians are urban residents.
   a. 25 percent
   b. 50 percent
   c. 60 percent
   d. 75 percent
   e. 90 percent

3. Which of the following were reasons why people were drawn to preindustrial cities?
   a. economic incentive
   b. the prospect of a more interesting and stimulating life
   c. the comparative safety of life in the city compared with the small town
   d. a and b
   e. all of the above

4. Industrialization
   a. made it possible for most people to live in cities
   b. made it necessary for most people to live in cities
   c. depends on specialization
   d. all of the above
   e. none of the above

5. According to the U.S. census, in order to qualify as a city a community must have at least _____ residents.
   a. 2,500
   b. 20,000
   c. 50,000
   d. 75,000
   e. 100,000

6. If a locale has a population of more than 2,500 demographers term it a(n) _____.
   a. urban place
   b. urban area
   c. community
   d. city
   e. village

7. The area surrounding a city whose inhabitants depend on the central city for jobs, recreation, media, and a sense of community constitute the city's:
   a. metropolitan area
   b. sphere of influence
   c. metropolis
   d. zone of transition
   e. zone of influence

8. An area counts as a Standard Metropolitan Statistical Area if it:
   a. has a central city of 50,000 or more
   b. is surrounded by a county in which 75 percent of those working in the county work in agriculture
   c. is surrounded by a county in which 15 percent of the workers commute to the central city for work
   d. a and c
   e. all of the above

9. Fixed-rail cities:
   a. made the center of the city the focal point
   b. are common in the western United States
   c. are more evenly spread out than the freeway metropolis
   d. all of the above
   e. none of the above

10. According to the Gallup Poll, most Americans preferred to live:
    a. in a city
    b. on a farm
    c. in a suburb or small town
    d. b and c
    e. none of the above

11. The theory of ethnic succession is associated most closely with:
    a. Park and Burgess
    b. Tönnies
    c. Durkheim
    d. Wirth
    e. none of the above

12. The degree of segregation or integration of a neighborhood is measured by a(n):
    a. index of similarity
    b. index of dissimilarity
    c. index of status characteristics
    d. index of ethnic characteristics
    e. none of the above

13. Guest and Weed:
    a. argued that Park and Burgess were discussing individual upward mobility
    b. argued that the status inequality between groups seems to be the primary neighborhood barrier
    c. found evidence that would discredit the theory of Park and Burgess
    d. a and b
    e. all of the above

14. Research on anomie in urban areas has found that:
    a. considerable support exists for anomie theories
    b. urbanites typically maintain close attachments to others
    c. anomie is characteristic of most urbanites
    d. a and c
    e. none of the above

15. Macro studies of crowding have found that:
    a. considerable support exists for the "psychic overload" theory
    b. city people are more prone to alcoholism and mental illness than are rural people
    c. neighborhoods with high population density had much higher rates of pathology than did less dense neighborhoods
    d. all of the above
    e. none of the above

16. The micro studies of Gove and others found that:
    a. there is little support for micro theories of crowding
    b. people in crowded homes had poorer mental health
    c. members of crowded homes had poorer social relations
    d. b and c
    e. none of the above

17. The concepts of *Gemeinschaft* and *Gesellschaft* are associated with:
    a. Park and Burgess
    b. Tönnies
    c. Durkheim
    d. Wirth
    e. Guest and Weed

18. Characteristics of *Gesellschaft* include:
    a. people are united only by self-interest
    b. group members share little agreement about the norms and deviance is common
    c. human relationships are fleeting and manipulative
    d. all of the above
    e. none of the above

19. Durkheim argued that:
    a. a primary consequence of urbanization was the breakdown of order
    b. urbanites live in a state of anomie
    c. rural areas have higher crime rates than urban areas
    d. a and b
    e. all of the above

20. Research by Gove et al. on crowding found:
    a. child care in crowded homes was poor
    b. the effects of crowding began to show up only when there were more than two people per room in a household
    c. people responded to crowding by withdrawing mentally and physically
    d. a and c
    e. all of the above

Essay

1. A. Define urbanization. (knowledge)
    B. Describe some characteristics of preindustrial cities. (comprehension)
    C. Discuss the interplay between urbanization and modernization. (analysis)

2. A. Name Park and Burgess's theory. (knowledge)
    B. Explain this theory. (comprehension)
    C. Show how recent research studies have (or have not) supported this theory. (analysis)

3. Discuss some characteristics of preindustrial cities and show how these characteristics limited their size.

4. Distinguish between Tönnies's concepts of *Gemeinschaft* and *Gesellschaft*.

5. Discuss macro and micro theories of crowding and cite relevant research findings.

Answers

Completion

1. urbanization
2. modernization
3. succession
4. disease
5. industrialization
6. specialization
7. urban place
8. 50,000
9. metropolis
10. sphere of influence
11. fixed-rail
12. freeway metropolises
13. Park, Burgess
14. economic, status
15. status inequality
16. Durkheim, Wirth
17. micro, macro
18. *Gemeinschaft*
19. industrial
20. suburb

Multiple Choice

1. e
2. d
3. d
4. d
5. c
6. a
7. b
8. d
9. a
10. c
11. a
12. b
13. b
14. b
15. e
16. d
17. b
18. d
19. d
20. d

CHAPTER TWENTY

The Organizational Age

Overview

After describing the characteristics of formal organizations, this chapter uses examples of the military, private business, and government to describe the process of centralization in nineteenth-century organizations. It then discusses Weber's concept of rational bureaucracy and the rational system approach. This approach is contrasted wih the natural system approach to the study of formal organizations. Chapter 20 next considers the process of decentralization in private business and highlights the theories of Blau and Thompson. The chapter closes with a look at the increasing centralization in government.

Capsule Summary

Formal (or **rational**) **organizations** differ from older forms of organization in that they apply **reason** to the **problems** of **management**. **Characteristics** of **formal organizations** include the following: a clear **statement** of **goals**, operating **principles** and **procedures** for **pursuing** these goals, **trained leaders**, clear lines of **communication** and authority, and **written communication** and **records**. During the **nineteenth century**, formal organizations emerged in such diverse areas as the **military**, **private industry**, and the **government**.

    Max Weber termed these organizations **rational bureaucracies**. His approach, often termed the **rational system approach**, emphasizes the **official** and **intended** characteristics of an organization and focuses on the processes of **goal displacement**, **goal conflict**, and **informal relations among members**. Rather than opposing one another, these two appoaches are really complementary views.

    Although the nineteenth century saw the centralization of business and industry, more recently the trend in these organizations has been one of **decentralizaton**. This process relies on **autonomous divisions**, **differentiation**, and **discretion**. The theories of **Blau** and **Thompson**, which have focused on this process, have led to considerable empirical research.

    Ironically, while private **businesses** have become increasingly **decentralized**, **governments** have tended to become even more **centralized**. When applied to government, the terms **bureaucracy** and **bureaucrat** have taken on a negative connotation in the minds of many people. Because governments are not as vulnerable as private organizations, recent critics have suggested that they too should be subject to objective evaluations of performance.

Key Concepts

You should be able to explain the concepts listed here and be prepared to cite several examples of each concept.

Formal organization 584
Rational organization 584
Vertical integration 589
Functional division 589
Spoils system 592
Bureaucracy 593
Rational system approach 594
Goal displacement 595

Natural system approach 595
Goal conflict 596
Span of control 600
Diversified organization 600
Autonomous division 600
Decentralization 601
Management by objectives 602
Discretion 602

Key Theories

You should be able to explain the assumptions of these theories and, when applicable, cite related research findings.

Weber: rational system approach
Natural system approach
Blau: theory of organization
Thompson: decentralization, discretion, and coalition formation

Completion

1. The _____ organization applies reason to the problems of management.

2. During the _____ century the first large formal organizations were created.

3. The political practice of giving public offices to the supporters of the winning politician is termed the _____.

4. For Weber the term *bureaucracy* was inseparable from the term _____.

5. The rational system approach emphasizes the _____ and _____ characteristics of organizations.

6. The _____ system approach emphasizes the informal and unintended characteristics of organizations.

7. _____ occurs when organizations change their goals in pursuit of survival.

8. _____ occurs when different groups within an organization tend to pursue different goals.

9. The _____ system approach argues that the overriding goal of organizations is to survive.

10. The limit on the number of people a given person can supervise effectively is termed the _____.

11. The key element in the decentralization of organizations is _____.

12. Blau argued that the _____ the organization, the greater the proportion of total resources that must be devoted to management.

13. Discretion involves both the _____ for making decisions and the _____ to carry them out.

14. The more serious the potential consequences of an error are perceived to be, the _____ willing people will be to assume discretion.

15. Recently business has _____, and government has become increasingly _____.

16. The strength of private bureaucracies is their _____.

17. The organization of military troops into small, identical units, each containing all military elements, is an example of a _____ system.

18. Parts of an organization, each of which includes a full set of functional divisions, are termed _____ divisions.

19. The dispersing of authority from a few central administrators to persons directly engaged in activities is termed _____.

20. A situation in which managers and subordinates agree on goals that subordinates will try to achieve is termed _____.

Multiple Choice

1. During the _____ century formal organizations developed in the military, business, and government.
   a. twentieth
   b. nineteenth
   c. eighteenth
   d. seventeenth
   e. sixteenth

2. Formal organizations differ from older forms of organization in that formal organizations:
   a. depend on a clear statement of goals
   b. possess clear lines of authority and communication
   c. use written records and communications
   d. a and c
   e. all of the above

3. Rational bureaucracy was first described by:
   a. Peter Blau
   b. Max Weber
   c. James Thompson
   d. Emile Durkheim
   e. none of the above

4. In the spoils system:
   a. the benefits of public office go to the supporters of winning politicians
   b. people are encouraged to make a career of government service
   c. people are prevented from making a career of government service
   d. a and b
   e. a and c

5. The _____ system approach emphasizes the informal and unintended characteristics of organizations:
   a. rational
   b. natural
   c. informal
   d. irrational
   e. unnatural

6. According to Weber, bureaucracy is based on:
   a. functional specialization
   b. a blurring of lines of authority
   c. managers promoted on the basis of the spoils system
   d. a and b
   e. all of the above

7. Criticisms of the rational approach include:
   a. the real lines of communication in organizations are not always the same as those on the organizational chart
   b. all members always pursue the same goals
   c. the approach is limited
   d. a and c
   e. all of the above

8. According to the natural system approach, the overriding goal of organizations is to:
   a. specialize
   b. self-distrust
   c. survive
   d. diversify
   e. a and d

9. The situation termed _____ may occur when different groups within an organization tend to pursue different goals than the goals of the organization.
   a. goal conflict
   b. goal displacement
   c. decentralization
   d. functional integration
   e. none of the above

10. A company that is _____ controls each step in the process of bringing its products to the consumer.
   a. horizontally integrated
   b. decentralized
   c. vertically integrated
   d. functionally disintegrated
   e. none of the above

11. When the March of Dimes changed its focus from the elimination of polio to the elimination of birth defects, it exhibited:
   a. functional integration
   b. goal displacement
   c. goal conflict
   d. horizontal integration
   e. rationalization

12. A major shortcoming of the rational system approach is that it fails to emphasize:
   a. the formal structure
   b. goal displacement
   c. the organizational blueprint
   d. b and c
   e. all of the above

13. The limit of the number of people that a given person can supervise effectively is termed the:
   a. functional limit
   b. span of control
   c. vertical integration limit
   d. supervisory sphere
   e. none of the above

14. In order to survive, the DuPont company had to institute:
    a. centralization
    b. functional limits
    c. autonomous divisions
    d. supervisory spheres
    e. all of the above

15. In his theory of administrative growth, Blau argued that:
    a. as organizations become less diversified, the size of administrative components increases relative to the size of other components
    b. the smaller the organization, the greater the proportion of total resources that must be devoted to management function
    c. organizational growth causes differentiation
    d. a and c
    e. all of the above

16. Thompson argued that members of an organization will accept discretion when:
    a. they believe they cannot adequately control conditions affecting decisions
    b. they do not share the responsibility of that decision with others
    c. the decision involves forces outside the organization
    d. a and c
    e. all of the above

17. Which of the following statements is/are true?
    a. as governmental organizations have grown larger, they have decentralized
    b. centralization has dominated governmental organizations, and decentralization has dominated private organizations
    c. as governmental organizations have grown larger, they have become more centralized
    d. b and c
    e. none of the above

18. Breaking an organization into smaller units on the basis of specialized activities is termed:
    a. decentralization
    b. natural system approach
    c. geographical division
    d. functional divisions
    e. none of the above

19. When the official goals of an organization are ignored or changed, it is termed:
    a. goal conflict
    b. goal rejection
    c. goal replacement
    d. goal displacement
    e. none of the above

20. The rational system approach emphasizes:
   a. the intended characteristics of the organization
   b. the informal characteristics of the organization
   c. the unintended characteristics of the organization
   d. b and c
   e. a and b

Essay

1. A. Name the two approaches to the study of bureaucracy. (knowledge)
   B. Explain each of these approaches. (comprehension)
   C. Contrast these approaches. (analysis)

2. A. Define formal organization. (knowledge)
   B. Describe four official and intended characteristics of formal organizations. (comprehension)
   C. Apply these characteristics to the military, government, and/or private industry. (application)

3. Describe the characteristics of formal organizations that distinguish them from older forms of organization.

4. Using the examples in the text, trace the development of formal organization in the military, private business, and government.

5. Explain the process of decentralization. Discuss *either* Blau's theory *or* Thompson's theory on the decentralization process.

Answers

Completion

1. formal or rational
2. nineteenth
3. spoils system
4. rationality
5. official and intended
6. natural
7. goal displacement
8. goal conflict
9. natural
10. span of control
11. discretion
12. larger
13. responsibility, authority
14. less
15. decentralized, centralized
16. vulnerability
17. divisional
18. autonomous
19. decentralization
20. management of objectives

Multiple Choice

1. b	11. b
2. e	12. b
3. b	13. b
4. e	14. c
5. b	15. c
6. a	16. b
7. d	17. d
8. c	18. d
9. a	19. d
10. c	20. a

CHAPTER TWENTY-ONE

Collective Behavior and Social Movements

Overview

This chapter, written by William Sims Bainbridge, offers a conceptual framework for analyzing collective behavior and social movements. It starts with a description of this framework and distinguishes among parallel behavior, collective behavior, and social movements. It describes the various forms of collective behavior—panics, crazes, and riots—and offers in-depth accounts of historical examples of each. Chapter 21 then discusses the rise of Nazism as an example of a successful mass movement. It concludes with a description of the rise of a successful elite movement, the spaceflight movement, in which the author presents material drawn from his research and lifelong interest in rocketry and spaceflight.

Capsule Summary

Often groups of people engage in **unusual behavior** in an attempt to **encourage**, **prevent**, or **react** to **social change**. When this behavior occurs **spontaneously**, with **little or no organization or planning**, it is termed **collective behavior**. When it is of **longer duration**, **planned**, and **organized**, it is termed a **social movement**. **Parallel behavior**, on the other hand, lacks the element of **group interaction**, which characterizes both **collective behavior** and **social movements**. Through increased focused interaction, **parallel behavior** may be transformed into **collective behavior**, a **social movement**, and ultimately a **social institution**. In reality, however, few collective actions succeed in this fashion.

    Collective behavior includes **crazes** (or **fads**), **panics**, and **riots**. **Crazes** occur when a number of people rush toward something they desire. Frisbees, Hula Hoops, and tulips have all been the focus of crazes. **Panics**, on the other hand, occur when people flee from real or imagined danger. Often, as in the case of the "War of the Worlds" broadcast or the Barseback incident, reactions to panics are overestimated. **Riots** occur when a crowd threatens or attacks persons or property. The Nika uprising and the case of the Luddites are examples of **riots**.

    The **Nazi movement** is an example of a successful **mass movement**. To grow, mass movements rely on a **natural constituency** from which to draw members and an **internal society** capable of attracting and incorporating new members. Social conditions and the political structure of Germany after World War I provided the Nazis with both. Drawing on its strength in the middle class, Nazism grew from an obscure movement among many other movements to a mass movement that temporarily controlled and dominated an entire society.

    Not all **successful social movements** are **mass movements** drawing their support from **oppressed groups** or a **discontented middle class**. Some, like the **spaceflight movement**, are

elite movements that draw their support from the **dominant social** and **political structures**. Bainbridge's study of this movement drew on previously published accounts of the history of rocketry and his own lifelong interest in the subject. Through his research, he was able to show how this movement developed around an **opportunity** and grew into a successful movement. By showing how highly dedicated and gifted people can use opportunities to further their own interests, his research has called into question some of the assumptions of **technological determination**.

Key Concepts

Be prepared to explain the following concepts and be able to cite several examples of each concept.

Collective behavior 610	Riot 619
Social movement 611	Internal society 624
Social institution 612	Interactive model 634
Parallel behavior 613	First-generation leader 635
Craze 614	Second-generation leader 635
Mania 614	Ideologue 636
Panic 615	Executive 636
Crowd behavior 616	Technological determinism 637
Summary event 617	

Key Examples

Rather than discussing specific theories or contributions, this chapter offers a conceptual framework for understanding collective behavior and social movements. You should be thoroughly familiar with this framework and be able to apply it to specific situations. You should also be able to identify these examples, explain the course of events that occurred, and show how they illustrate the various characterisics of collective behavior and social movements.

Flagpole sitting
Tulipomania
"War of the Worlds"
Barseback incident
Nika uprising
Luddites
Nazi movement
Spaceflight movement

Completion

1. Flagpole sitting is an example of a phenomenon termed a(n) _____ or _____.

2. Behavior that tends to be brief, episodic, and organized is termed _____.

3. Organized groups dedicated to _____ or _____ social change are termed social movements.

4. Situations in which terrified people attempt to flee danger are termed _____.

5. In a _____, people rush toward something they all desire.

6. A hostile outburst of collective behavior in which a crowd of people threatens or attacks other persons or property is termed a _____.

7. Collective behavior tends to be brief, episodic, and _____.

8. _____ are sustained by organization and planning, and they often endure for a long time.

9. _____ occurs when each person is doing the same thing for the same reason but each is doing it alone.

10. The War of the Worlds and the Barseback incident are examples of _____.

11. Panic is most likely when an ambiguous threat is seen as _____.

12. A concrete representation of a vague but intense social and emotional situation is termed a _____.

13. A segment of the population for the mass movement to represent that does not have effective representation is termed a(n) _____.

14. Systems of beliefs and values that passively influence a social movement are termed _____.

15. A cohesive network of social relationships within a movement is termed a(n) _____.

16. Conditions necessary for the growth of a mass movement include an internal society and a _____.

17. Social disorganization on a large scale often leads to _____ on a small scale.

18. The type of leader who functions to build and guide a social enterprise is termed a(n) _____.

19. The spaceflight movement drew its interest and support primarily from the _____ classes.

20. _____ is the belief that technological change is automatic and that when the time is right for the next step forward it will occur.

Multiple Choice

1. Actions may be related to social change when:
   a. the action may be aimed at preventing social change
   b. the action may be undertaken to cause social change
   c. the action itself may be a social change
   d. a and b
   e. all of the above

2. Primary reasons for doing sociology include:
   a. to understand the interplay between the individual and society
   b. to prove that we are entirely creations of our society and that our history determines our destiny
   c. to make social life less mysterious
   d. a and c
   e. all of the above

3. In order for a behavior to be classified as collective behavior:
   a. the individuals must have no influence over each other
   b. there must be little or no planning
   c. the action may be taken by lone individuals as well as groups
   d. a and c
   e. all of the above

4. Collective behavior and social movements differ:
   a. in the degree of planning
   b. in their length and duration
   c. in their degree of organization
   d. a and c
   e. all of the above

5. When people are doing the same thing for the same reason but each person is doing it alone, it is referred to as:
   a. collective behavior
   b. parallel behavior
   c. a social movement
   d. a reactionary movement
   e. isolated behavior

6. In a _____ a group of people rush toward something they desire.
   a. panic
   b. craze
   c. riot
   d. parallel behavior
   e. none of the above

7. In a _____ people rush away from something they all fear.
   a. panic
   b. craze
   c. riot
   d. parallel behavior
   e. none of the above

8. The cases of the Luddites and the Nika uprising were examples of:
   a. crazes
   b. riots
   c. panics
   d. parallel behavior
   e. none of the above

9. A concrete representation of a vague but intense social and emotional situation is termed a(n) _____.
   a. natural constituency
   b. internal society
   c. summary event
   d. precipitating incident
   e. precipitating event

10. In a social movement a cohesive network of social relationships capable of attracting and incorporating large numbers of new members is termed a(n):
   a. natural constituency
   b. internal society
   c. collective coalition
   d. ideological supporters
   e. none of the above

11. Conditions that are necessary for the growth of a mass movement include:
    a. a strong ideology to recruit new members
    b. a vigorous internal society
    c. a natural constituency
    d. b and c
    e. all of the above

12. The spaceflight movement:
    a. began as parallel behavior
    b. was created by oppressed groups
    c. had a strong natural constituency from which to draw support
    d. all of the above
    e. none of the above

13. Successful social movements:
    a. are always mass movements
    b. are always created by oppressed groups
    c. always draw their strength from the misery of some natural constituency
    d. all of the above
    e. none of the above

14. Which of the following statements is/are not true?
    a. social movements are always drawn from oppressed people
    b. ideology plays a very active role in the formation of most social movements
    c. almost all social movements are successful
    d. all of the above
    e. none of the above

15. Smelser termed the type of leader who invents and spreads ideas the _____ leader.
    a. ideologue
    b. executive
    c. expressive
    d. instrumental
    e. none of the above

16. Technological determinists:
    a. argue that changes in technology are the cause of all social change
    b. argue that technological change is self-generating
    c. emphasize that unusually talented people often speed up the pace of innovation
    d. a and b
    e. all of the above

17. The Nazi movement's greatest strength was in the _____ class.
    a. lower
    b. working
    c. middle
    d. upper

18. Bainbridge gathered most of his data on the spaceflight movement from:
    a. interviews
    b. participant observation
    c. books
    d. visits to rocket installations
    e. none of the above

19. Which of the following is a typical sequence of events in a successful social movement?
    a. parallel behavior, collective behavior, social movement, social institution
    b. social movement, collective behavior, parallel behavior
    c. social movement, collective behavior, social institution
    d. parallel behavior, social institution, social movement
    e. parallel behavior, collective behavior, social institution, social movement

20. The rise of Nazism was fostered by:
    a. a strong ideology that helped recruit new members at the beginning of the movement
    b. the political system that encouraged the development of many political parties
    c. its appeal to the lower class
    d. all of the above
    e. a and b

Essay

1. A. Explain the interactive model. (comprehension)
   B. Apply the interactive model to the spaceflight movement. (application)
   C. Compare and contrast the spaceflight movement with the Nazi movement. (analysis)

2. A. Name three types of collective behavior. (knowledge)
   B. Give examples of these three types. (comprehension)
   C. Compare and contrast collective behavior and social movement. (analysis)

3. Discuss the criteria that must be met for a behavior to be considered collective behavior.

4. Using an example (real or fictitious), trace the sequence of events that occur as parallel behavior is transformed into a social institution.

5. Using the material presented in this chapter, respond to the following question: "Do we make our history or does it make us?"

Answers

Completion
1. craze, fad
2. collective behavior
3. causing, preventing
4. panics
5. craze
6. riot
7. unorganized
8. social movements
9. parallel behavior
10. panics
11. immediate
12. summary event
13. natural constituency
14. ideologies
15. internal society
16. natural constituency
17. increased social organization
18. executive
19. middle and upper
20. technological determinism

Multiple Choice
1. e
2. d
3. b
4. e
5. b
6. b
7. a
8. b
9. c
10. b
11. d
12. a
13. e
14. d
15. a
16. d
17. c
18. c
19. a
20. b

Review and Special Project

Review

This section focused on changes brought about by modernization. It described population trends, urban growth and development, the centralization and decentralization of organizations, and collective behavior and social movements.

Special Project

Rapid shifts in population can cause changes in society. Special Topic 6 focused on many of the changes brought about by the "baby boom." During the 1960s, colleges and universities experienced growth and change as the baby boom generation entered college. During the 1970s and early 1980s, many colleges experienced declining enrollment among traditional college students. This decline necessitated further change.

You might wish to study the impact that this group and its passing had on some aspects of your college or university. Possible areas to investigate include the following suggestions.

1. Demographic changes in the composition of students and faculty (age, race, sex, marital status, and so on).
2. Building expansion or changes in the use of physical space.
3. Curriculum changes and changes in degree requirements.
4. The increase (or decrease) of different categories of students in specific majors or programs.
5. Increased (or decreased) interest and participation in social movements and political activism.
6. Increased (or decreased) interest and participation in student organizations such as sororities and fraternities.
7. Changes in the organizational structure of some components of the school.

Possible sources of information and data for the topic you choose could include student profiles and demographic data available from administrative offices; interviews with faculty, administrators, former and current students; college catalogs; maps; curriculum information; sorority and fraternity records; and college newspapers. Of course, the changes you will observe are the result of the complex interaction of societal changes that have occurred over the past two decades. You will want to incorporate these changes into your explanation of changes on your campus.